Planning
Your Family Staycation

Fun Ideas for Your
At-Home Summer Vacation

Denise D. Witmer

Planning Your Family Staycation: Fun Ideas for Your At-Home Summer Vacation

ISBN 978-1-105-60115-6
Published by Lulu

To my husband Scott

and my daughters

Bri, Gigi and Mari

About the Author

Denise D. Witmer is a recognized writer of parenting and family books and websites including her book, *The Everything Parent's Guide to Raising a Successful Child* and creating About.com's Parenting Teens site and publishing its articles and resources since 1997. Her site and advice has been featured in US News and World Report, Better Homes and Garden's Raising Teens Magazine and USA Today online.

Ms. Witmer has been a 'professional parent' at a Childrens' Home in Pennsylvania from 1988 to 2006. Throughout that time, she has taken many group and family vacations and successfully put together countless staycation activities and day trips. She was very active in child and teen development and helped create their independent living programs. She is trained in PET (Parent Effectiveness Training), STEP (Support and Training for Exceptional Parents) and is the mother of three children. She also completed graduate courses at Penn State University for child and social psychology.

You can read more about Denise's current and past work on her website:

http://www.denisedwitmer.com

**About.com is part of the New York Times Company*

Table of Contents

What Is a Staycation?

A staycation is defined as 'a vacation spent at home doing enjoyable activities or visiting local attractions.'

"*There is nothing like staying at home for real comfort.*" ~ Jane Austen

What Staycations Are Not

A family staycation is not a time to make home repairs or improvements. There will be a time to do that and you can even take vacations days from work to complete those tasks if that is what you need. But if you are planning a staycation with your family, really plan to be on vacation with your family because that is what it is – a real vacation – you just get to sleep in your own bed.

Why Stay at Home for Vacation?

Today's family is overextended. We work long hours, our kids are in many activities and money flows out the door as fast as it can flow in. This makes for a ragged family schedule and a tight budget. Two excellent reasons many families who enjoy staycations give for not traveling away from their home to enjoy themselves and relax.

Somewhere down the line, our generation of families has gotten away from our homes being a haven of camaraderie, rest and peace. A well-planned and fun family staycation can change that for you and your family. Using your everyday living space will not turn your special times into humdrum stints lacking any real fun and laughter. Quite the opposite! Your staycation will show you how to turn your home and local area into an exciting and inviting place for your family vacation time.

Gas prices are off the charts. The thought of paying those prices to take long trips is one reason many families are giving for not taking a vacation. The cost of 'getting there' has simply risen to levels where people are just not going. This has affected all kinds of prices, from airfare to the price of a cup of coffee at the rest stop. And we aren't talking just a few cents. When parents add up airfare costs for a five person family, they begin to wonder if they should just pay off their teen's braces instead.

Quite a few families are facing a parent being out of work or getting paid less because of pay. Having less money means tightening the budget and travel vacations are usually the first to get cut. In these cases I'm hoping the staycation tips in this book will help you recharge so you can look forward to brighter opportunities.

Does any of this mean you should never go on a regular family vacation where you travel to another location? No way! Believe it or not, staycations can even make travel vacations better by strengthening your family bonds and actually 'teaching' your family how to have fun together without placing all of those expectations on your family while you are on an away trip.

More reasons people are staying at home to vacation:

- Global warming, green people prefer not to tax the environment.
- The crowds are overwhelming.
- Health issues keep some families close to home.
- Some families simply prefer to stay at home.
- The aggravation of getting there makes being there no fun.

Staycation Trends

Much to the destination travel industry's chagrin, the family staycation is a trend that is strengthening year-after-year. Since as early as 2008, families have been taking their time off of work and spending it at home, going on local day trips and just enjoying each other without all of the hassle of traveling to faraway places. Now we have coined the phrase 'staycation' and it was added to Merriam Webster's Collegiate Dictionary in 2009.

This brings us to the present. This is the time you and your family are thinking about enjoying a staycation. How has the current trend brought you here? Does it matter, really?

Whatever your budget concerns and monitory reasons for thinking about a staycation verses a vacation, I am going to bet that once you read through this book, you will come away with ideas and solutions that will not only make the current staycation you are planning loads of fun, but you will perpetuate the trend because of all the added benefits your family experiences.

A 2005 study by the Families and Work Institute found that up to one-third of employees who get paid vacation time do not use it all. Many cite not having the money to get away on a trip. They feel as if vacations can only happen if one can get away from home as well as work. Yet taking a break from work is a healthy way to tone down stress and build strong bonds with our family. Families who enjoy staycations can have the best of both worlds, they enjoy the health benefits of taking the time off of work that they've earned and they get to enjoy each other while building those bonds.

Embracing the Concept of a Staycation

Understanding the concept of a staycation starts with planning a vacation that has a start date and an end date where your home is your base of operations. During your staycation you will use your base as the place where you go from and return to after an activity, as the place to host an activity or as the place to simply relax. At your base of operations everyone will have access to new and favorite activities, a schedule of the staycation plans and the ability to relax in a way that they enjoy, like listening to their own music, watching a favorite television show or enjoying a book they are reading.

During a staycation, you and your family become tourists to your local area. Finding entertaining activities in your local area that you may have never even looked for is one of the biggest benefits to going on staycation. How many times have your driven by an amusement park, museum or even the local library without considering its ability to help create a wonderful experience for your family? Staycations are the perfect time to explore some of those possible experiences.

Time Well Spent

Time together as a family is always well spent if we put forth an effort to engage in activities together and enjoy each other's company. Keep in mind that this time, your staycation, is time with your family doing things together–even if it is just relaxing.

Try and switch up your normal routine during your staycation, don't go to the same restaurants or movie theaters. Your staycation is an opportunity for your family to try new things in your local area. For instance, if when you choose to go out to eat you eat at the local Chinese restaurant, maybe this time you could try the Japanese restaurant or your family can see a live show at the local theater instead of attending a movie. By trying new things, you will make the staycation more exciting and you may find some new favorite things to do together. You'll remember this time together forever.

Money Well Saved

When businesses cut the budget in the office it means that workers have to cut their budgets at home. This translates to workers getting rid of what isn't necessary. The car will make it another year, we begin to look at more and more sales flyers for grocery store items and we need to cut back on the luxuries. Family travel vacations are one of the luxuries that seem to be cut first. They are really becoming a financial extravagance for many families.

That is where staycations come in. While you will not be on a tropical island sunbathing in the sand – unless you live there – you will be enjoying time off of work, time with those you love and time to explore the area you live in.

In the section on planning your staycation, I talk more about creating a budget with lots of tips. But, there are a couple of points I want to state here: You don't need to spend a lot of money to have a great time with your family. You also don't need to be poor to think about enjoying a staycation. Everyone likes to save money when they can.

START YOUR STAYCATION PLANNING

"*A good plan is like a road map: it shows the final destination and usually the best way to get there.*" ~ H. Stanley Judd

Planning for your vacation at home will help you resist falling into everyday habits that can ruin a good staycation. It will break you from the not-doing-much routine of watching television and get you and your family out and about in your local area. Also when you make the time to plan out your itinerary, you will put yourself in the vacation mindset, something that can be hard for first-time staycationers especially.

Be Organized, Right From the Get-Go

You cannot create the perfect plan for your family's staycation if you are unable to find the flyers you picked up the visitor's center. It is impossible to fit planning tasks into your already busy schedule if you are not organized.

Start organizing by designating one spot where everything about your staycation will be kept. This could be a desk drawer or like in my world, it's a large tote bag. In this bag I have

- A 3-inch 3-ring binder that holds pocket pages and paper;
- Maps of the area;
- An address book;
- Tourism magazines.

I use the binder to keep notes of where the family wants to go, dates set for staycations and things that need to happen before the staycation starts. I also keep all of the pamphlets that I found on places we would like to go during our staycation. Not all of the pamphlets I have picked up are in the binder, only ones that were voted on and accepted – then maybe some others in case there is extra time. I also have an address book to tape business cards and clip advertisements in. This is in case we ever want to check a place out again at a later date; I will have the information without having to keep the pamphlet.

I'm always picking up maps of places I'm in, even my local area. Yes, you can use a GPS system in your car, but maps of local areas and businesses have fun facts or coupons on them. They are worth collecting, so if you see one, grab it. Tourism magazines of your local area are fun to collect and often have great ideas in them as well.

Paper is not the only thing you will need to keep organized. All of the websites you are using to research should be kept in one file under your bookmarks. Don't try to remember any of it – that is too stressful – just bookmark as you go to use when you need them. You can delete the sites you don't need later.

Do the Legwork

Now that you have a place to put it, go get some stuff to fill it. Visit your local library, visitor's center, community center and take a trip into the lobby of the nearest hotel. Pick any and all tourist magazines, activity pamphlets, local maps and event flyers. Check with your local newspaper to see if they publish a week's activities section and what day it is published. You'll want to pick one up for the week of your staycation.

When you are doing the leg work, don't spend too much time thinking. You can read over everything at home and discard anything your family isn't interested in there. Unless you have questions about places you are looking for, spend as little time as possible grabbing as many free information brochures as possible.

Next, head out to visit all of your area restaurants. Go to sit down restaurants as well as take out and bar and grills. Stop at little bistros and sandwich shops as well. When there ask if you can have a copy of their menu – most have something you can take home even if they don't deliver – and ask if they have delivery service. Mark the menus that have delivery and take them all home and save them in your tote.

Finding Local Resources

The visitor's center in your area has a plethora of flyers, maps and advertisements all about everything in the area. And the best part about this information is that it is free. You can build your own guide book by choosing things your family will want to do and bringing them to the planning session. Bring more than you think you will need. Actually, since you live in the area, why not take one of each? You don't have to fit it all in during your first staycation, but you can always plan more day trips on the weekend or keep them for the next staycation.

Your community center for your town or city will have the schedule for your week. There may be classes, craft shows, community theater events or an art event at the local community college going on that your family may want to participate in or just go and see. Belonging to a community gives a sense of security to kids and families. Plus, when you attend community events, you'll get to know people in your area better.

Choosing the Dates of Your Staycation

Choosing the dates of the family staycation is more easily done by the adults of the family taking into consideration all that their children may be involved it. If you normally take a certain week off during the summer – by all means, do the same for your staycation. If there was something you wanted to do during your staycation that only happens at a certain time of year, then that is when you should plan it.

As the workers in the household, you know best when you can fit in some time off. It is important that when you start planning your staycation, you have the dates set, as you kids and others will have to make plans around it. Decide before your family planning meeting.

In my mind, a 5-day staycation a week off sandwiched between two normal weekends where we do normal weekend things. The plans that follow are based on this premise. However, they are easily changed to fit your staycation days. You can simply add the weekend days to your schedule and plan out a longer staycation or shorten to a three day plan if needed.

Get the Whole Family in on the Plan

Planning fun things to do is fun to do. The possibilities are endless and all should be explored. Give your kids and spouse a heads up that you will be having a family meeting to discuss your staycation plans. Between now and then they should think about things they want to do during your staycation and bring those ideas to the meeting. The planning meeting is not rushed. It is a relaxing and fun look at all of the possibilities, with the understanding that not all decisions are made in one meeting.

Before the meeting you will want to create the structure for a workable family staycation plan. A workable family staycation includes time to go out and try new things, time to enjoy personal endeavors and time to simply relax. Without these three things, your staycation will fall flat. Think about it for a minute. If all you do is go out and find new things in your area to do, you will return back to work exhausted and unfulfilled. This is often why people who come back to work after a vacation exclaim, "I need a vacation after my vacation!" They simply packed so much into their days off that they forgot to relax and give themselves the time to unwind. Do not plan your staycation like this.

Creating the structure of your staycation means you will implement the timing of what your family will be doing at any specific time. Print a calendar of the week from your computer for this task to start and then transfer it to the staycation schedule that the whole family will be able to see. While the activities have not been decided on, you do know that you do not want to do three day trips in a row – or that you may only want to do only one day trip and two evenings out. Having a well-defined structure for your staycation will help your family pick appropriate activities to fill the structure.

Give your kids an opportunity to share their ideas. You'll want to start by giving them a heads up as to what type of ideas you are looking for and then a few days to puzzle it out before your family meeting. You can suggest they write it down so they don't forget. You could even place a piece of paper with Staycation Ideas written across the top and places where they can use it.

Now if you have done your leg work, you have information and pamphlets to share with your kids. If you do that while they are thinking of ideas, they will have thought some things through before the meeting starts – which means you won't have to start at square one. This can do one of two things: One, you child will get excited about all the different things your will do on your staycation. Two, your child will get their heart set on doing one particular thing that you may or may not be able to do during your staycation. So you may need to warn them that ideas are not the plan, everyone will need to be flexible about your family staycation plan until it is set.

During the meeting, give someone the secretaries position and they should list all of the ideas your family has thought up – many of which will be going out type of activities. Mark off which ones are simply not possible at this time for whatever reason. Now you have cut the list down to all possible staycation activities. Define each activity by the time and type and make a list of 'like' activities. For instance 'going bowling' is an activity that can be done in a couple of hours during the afternoon or evening, while 'going to the beach' is a day trip. But both of these activities get you out of the house. You'll want to schedule in stay-at-home activities as well.

When you have your lists, you can fill in the open spots on the calendar. If there is more than one activity for a spot, you should vote on which activity your family would like to do. Every family member gets a vote. As you vote, take the activities that won and fit them into their spots on calendar. Use a pencil and have an eraser available. This will give you a working sketch of what your family staycation will look like. Remind everyone that this is subject to change as you try and work out the details.

Create a Staycation Schedule

While making a schedule may seem contrary to popular vacation beliefs, it really will keep your staycation organized and easier for you – the staycation wizard – to keep everything flowing without the stress it takes to keep it all in your head or on a hundred different lists that you are libel to lose. And because it is kept in an area that everyone can see, it will keep the whole family abreast of what you will be doing during the week.

Use a brightly colored poster board and add stickers so your kids can help decorate the schedule. Use markers to write out what you will be during the week.

Make a column for each day plus two: one for Ideas and Activities and the first one for marking off the times of the day. This column is for those things that you can do, but aren't scheduled into a time.

Make a row across the daily columns for the times of the day and the top one for titling the Days of the Week.

Add a set of five paper clips to the top of the board. This is to clip messages and notes to each other, ideas that are only maybes before they are added to the schedule or discarded, pamphlets of things you will be doing in case other family members want to look at them, etc.

Set Your Staycation Budget

Creating a budget for your staycation is similar to creating a budget for a vacation, except you get to save money on travel, gas, lodging and other expenses like car rentals. But just because you are staying in your home and saving quite a bit of money doesn't mean you can skip over creating a budget. You still have to figure out your expenses and come up with what you can afford to spend on your staycation. The cool thing is that if all you can afford to do is watch your own

DVDs, you can make an awesome movie marathon staycation just by purchasing popcorn and pizza with your grocery budget.

Here are some tips and a budget worksheet that can help:

- Remember, you are setting a budget for your vacation at home. The budget for a staycation is just like the budget for a regular vacation. You set your budget limits and go from there. So, first things first: What is your budget limit for your staycation? How much can you save to spend on your staycation?
- Keep day trip travel expense minimal. If you will be taking day trips, you will want to look at those expenses then decide what you will be doing with the rest of the funds on days you are planning on being at home. Don't forget to budget in the travel expenses that show up normally for day trips like gas, tickets and food for meals out.
- Understand that meals have to be eaten anyway. If you have separate funds for vacations and groceries, pull some of the grocery budget into your staycation budget. While you may spend more at the grocery store for staycation, you should still be able to cover much of it with your everyday weekly grocery funds.
- Get your children to earn their money. Do your children want to make extra money for your

staycation outings? Give them chores and jobs around the house for more funds.

- Pick the dates of your staycation wisely. Since you don't have to book your own home for your vacation, you can choose any date for your staycation. You may want to choose a time when the rates of your local hot spots are at a value time instead of when they are at their most expensive rates.
- Pack wisely for day trips and family outings. People often don't think of everything they need when going out for a day trip or outing like a hike or to a drive-in movie. Then, when they get to where they are going, they have to purchase extra things – like my usual, a sweatshirt if it gets cold. Plan and pack your day trips and outings keeping in mind all of the things you will need the entire time you are there.
- Bring water and snacks with you on outings and day trips. Nothing kills a budget like the hungry stomach of a child who has just spied a snack vendor. Keeping crackers and trail mix available will help keep you under budget.
- Set a budget for souvenirs. Souvenirs have a way of breaking a budget if you do not plan for them as day trip destinations often have very enticing gift shops. Set a price per person and stick to it. If your kids are old enough to understand budgeting, give them their allotted amount at the beginning of the week and let them budget the money themselves. They can

also add to their amount of money with their own funds.

- Keep track of your expenses. You will want to watch your expenses throughout your staycation to be sure that they stay in line with what you have budgeted. Make any necessary changes as you go for unforeseen circumstances.
- Write it down! Have a written account of what you budgeted and what you spent to keep for your next staycation planning.
- Book and pay for as much as possible in advance. This tip goes hand-in-hand with planning your staycation. While it may be easier to think that an at home vacation should be less planning and more spontaneity, really that isn't a benefit of a staycation. When you have a family, you need to plan your vacation whether it's at home or far away. The benefit comes when you save tons of money and stress less because you're enjoying your local area by following your staycation plan. Things you can pre-purchase that you might not otherwise think of:
- Use coupons and discounts for outings and day trips in your local area. Often day destinations will offer discount tickets sold by your local merchants. Look for these at your grocery and local department stores.
- Movie theaters have discounts on their gift certificates and cards. Check out what your

local movie theater offers and purchase them for your family staycation.

- Purchase items for your at-home theme days in advance from party stores sales and clearance sections. If you wait until the week before, you be stuck paying top dollar at a local retailer.
- Check out those grocery store fliers. Planning a special meal? Watch the grocery fliers up to two months in advance and pick up freezable or non-perishable items when they are on sale instead of waiting until the week of your staycation.

Resources:

Free Printable Budget Worksheet @ DollarTimes.com
http://www.dollartimes.com/download-and-print/
Site has worksheets you can use online and then print out – includes a blank one for any of your needs along with a family, vacation and pet budget worksheet.

Family Vacation Calculator @ CalcStuff.com
http://www.calcstuff.com/calcstuff/familyvacation.asp
The calculator will figure out your total costs and your cost by day.

Sample Staycation Schedules

Day One: Stay at Home/Theme Day or Activities

- Sleep-in
- Out for brunch/lunch
- Hobby, video game tournament or movie marathon activities
- (at-home afternoon and evening activities planned)
- Delivery menu dinner

Day Two: Day Trip #1

Day Three: Home Part of the Day

- Sleep in
- Continental breakfast
- Quiet activities
- Lunch out and afternoon activity out
- Delivery menu dinner or dinner out
- Family game night

Day Four: Day Trip #2

Day Five: Outdoor Activities

- Sleep in
- Continental Breakfast
- Go hiking, biking or to a park and picnic lunch
- Enjoy swimming or other outdoor activity in the afternoon
- Go out to a sit down restaurant
- Relax with a good book, calm music – or both!

Transforming Your Home Into a Vacation Get-Away

"*Laughter is an instant vacation.*" ~ Milton Berle

You do not need to renovate your home in order for it to feel like a place of refuge for you and your family during your staycation. The comforting feeling your family gets by being together will do that for you. Start with what you have, follow the suggestions in this chapter and your home will be a vacation get away that you will want to return to again and again.

What to Tell Your Friends, Neighbors and Bosses

First and foremost you will need to let the people who surround you every day that you are on vacation. You will not be answering the phone, email or be on your social network page. You and your family are going to be together, enjoying your time off from work without the hustle and bustle of life. And you will be doing this at home. But, just because you are at home does not in any way mean that you are available, because you are not. So, if they have a hard time reaching you, it's because you are on vacation.

Food Tips and Suggestions

One of the things about a vacation that adults love is the ability to eat out and not have to worry about cooking and cleaning up. Spending time at home on a staycation does not mean you have to do all of the chores you normally do every other day of the year. You simply need to be inventive with how you get your food chores done. Here are some tips you can use to make your staycation easier on you:

- Choose which meals to eat in your home and which ones to eat out. Don't limit your family to just going out for dinner during your staycation, many places for family meals have excellent breakfast and lunch fare – pancake restaurants come to mind.
- Make a meal plan that includes favorite snack foods. Plan for every meal, even if you think

you will be going out to a restaurant or ordering in. This is one area where you can purchase more than is needed as you will be able to use the foods in the near future if you were unable to eat them during the staycation. Take your plan and make a grocery shopping list. Write everything down including the staples you will need to make the food, recheck those in case you are running low. You do not want to have to run out to the store for something mid-staycation-week. Purchase all you need the week before staycation and place hands off signs on them if need be. Now you have what you will be eating and some extra this will be helpful if you have a change of plans during your week.

- Put together family continual breakfast meals before vacation starts. Purchase items your family likes to eat that they can fix themselves for a continental breakfast. Place enough items for one breakfast in a bag with the items needed to eat said breakfast, like cereal needs a paper bowl and plastic spoon – remember to try for no dishes! Each bag can represent one morning that you are having continental breakfast.
- One of the most un-fun chores in the kitchen is doing dishes. You can cut down on this chore by using paper plates and throw away utensils, ordering food in, make washing the dishes a family activity and of course, going out to eat.

- Instead of cooking a simple meal, make it the night's activity and cook something out of a specialty cookbook that you've wanted to try.
- Grilling and eating outside is a fun family activity can take away a lot of the kitchen chores and is perfect for a summer staycation activity. Make this one of your first staycation meals and pre-purchase ready-made salads and sides.
- Remember that you are not being graded on how clean your kitchen stays during your staycation. While you don't want a disaster in there, letting things go until after your family's evening activity – or even until morning – is doable.
- Ready-made foods are a godsend for staycations and make for stress free meal times. Anything that your family likes to eat that just needs thawed and heated is what you are looking to serve. Salads in a bag make a great side dish.
- When ordering food to eat in, strive to find places that have delivery in your local area. Order over the phone and have some fun with your family while you wait for it. Be sure to ask if they provide plastic utensils that you can discard after the meal.
- Scour your local coupon savers for restaurant and foodservice savings. Oft times we do not pay close attention to these types of savings in our own area, but they are a must-grab for staycation weeks.

Everyone Unplug!

We are a society of people who are connected. So much so, people can feel guilty if they do not answer their cellphones or update their statuses. If this is you, take a deep breath, you can do it. And you really must turn these things off for the majority of the time you are staycationing. You have to do this because if you continue to be connected to everything outside of your home and family, you will not be taking that much needed break. You will not be placing your family first and could hinder your ability to strengthen your bonds with them. You will still be in the outside world 'being busy' with outside concerns. Here are some tips on how to unplug:

- Remember to prepare everyone on your social network or cell phone call list about your staycation. Tell most people that you are going on vacation and you do not wish to be disturbed while you are vacationing with your family.
- Unplug your phones and turn off your cell phones. Place them all in a drawer where no one has immediate access and leave them there.
- Cover the family computer with a blanket so you don't even see it and put away any laptops in the home.
- Remind yourself you are not missing anything. Providing a relaxing atmosphere where you recharge means not allowing the outside world

to interrupt your time with your family during your staycation. The phone calls, emails and social network pages will be there when you get back.

- If totally unplugging from the world for the whole week is not an option, then you should unplug for 90% of the time. Mark a plugged-in time on your staycation schedule before your vacation starts, and then only during that time, you can do a quick check in. Get everyone on board with unplugging from the world outside of your family – your kids and teens too.
- If you are feeling an urge to get on the phone or computer, engage someone in your family in a game of cards or other group activity. This will help you get over the urge that is just a part of your everyday habit of being online or connected to your cell phone. Remind yourself that you can go back to it when you go back to work and your other daily routines.
- Try to unplug from your landline as well. Turning off the phone will help keep you distanced from others who may not be sensitive about the time you are trying to keep for your family. You should turn off the ringers and put the volume on a message machine to 0. Leave the message machine on and check it for emergency messages.

Unplugging from the world is not as hard as one might think. It takes a bit of a push in the beginning to deliberately not answer people who are trying to get a hold of you – but if you prepared them for your vacation, they will understand. It also takes some stamina to not fall into the habit of getting online or texting when you normally do. This is why you take precautions like turning the phone off and putting it away somewhere in a draw where you will not be tempted. If all else fails, remind yourself that your family is the most important thing in your life and then distract yourself by doing something with them.

Minimize Household Chores and Projects

In order for everyone to have fun, you will need to get rid of much of the work and chores that should be done around the house before your staycation begins. The best thing you can do is to hire someone to do it. Get a neighborhood teen to mow the lawn, call your local merry maids and have them come in and clean. If you are in the middle of a homeowner's project, either finish it the week before or cover it up so you can't see and won't think about it.

This is very important because if you don't do these things, you could sabotage your staycation. People who are in the habit of doing all day long have a hard time seeing something that needs to be done and ignoring it. But for your staycation week, your home is not something that you need to work on; it's a place of relaxation where you have chosen to recharge. Keep these things in mind:

- If you have a weekend project you want to do, wait until the first weekend you have off after your staycation. Do not ruin the time you have with your family with to-dos. Either put them on the done list before your staycation or save them for another time.
- Minimize daily chores by not being overly critical of getting all of them done during the week. You do not need to straighten your children's rooms or get a load of laundry through the washer and dryer. Leave it until after the staycation.
- Minimize the amount of dishes you have to wash by using a throw away set.
- Keep up with chores that are part of your weekly time schedule. For instance, put the trash out when the trash man is going to come and run the dishwasher nightly. Divvy up anything else to everyone who can help so as to not make one person do most of the work in the week.

Get Your Clothes Ready

When getting ready for a staycation, you want to avoid doing any type of chore, laundry included. So, you'll need to be prepared and have all of the laundry needed complete and ready for the staycation. One way is to pack as if you were actually going away on vacation. But that can be a hassle with kids and I prefer not to.

You could make a check list of what clothing items each person needs to have clean by the day before the staycation. This may cause some anxiety if your hampers are full, but not if you have kept up with the chore the week before the staycation.

During the week of the staycation, allow the laundry to pile up in the hampers and ignore it. If you find it hard not to look at the growing pile, put it into a closet you don't go in often. I have heard that people will take advantage of washer and dryers at hotels during their vacations so that they do not have to go home and do laundry on their first day back when they have to go back to work. But if you are sandwiching your staycation between two normal weekends, you'll have plenty of time for the chore then.

Getting young children ready in the morning can seem like a chore as well, but it is something that needs to be done during staycation. To make this chore easier, have out fits picked out and ready to put on for each day. Also, try not to rush your child. Take things are an easier pace than normal and there will be less stress.

Check Your Household and Personal Supplies

Much like when you are getting ready to go on a vacation, you will need to check that you have all of the household and personal items you need for your staycation. If you should forget one, you may have to run out to get it just when you were relaxing with a good book – no fun! Here is a checklist you can use:

Cleaning:

- Microfiber Cloths
- Bleach
- Baking Soda
- Vinegar
- Soap
- Office Supplies
- Paper
- Scotch Tape
- Packing tape
- Paper clips
- Rubber Bands

Bathroom & Personal

Pantry (continued)

- Toilet paper
- Band-Aids
- Antibacterial Ointment or Spray
- Feminine Hygiene Products
- Medicines
- Thermometer
- Toothpaste
- Shampoo
- Soap
- Sun Screen
- Aloe

- Rubbing Alcohol
- Hydrogen Peroxide
- Cough drops
- Q-Tips
- Shaving Cream
- Lotion
- Deodorant
- Razors

Kitchen

- Dishwasher Detergent
- Paper Towels
- Napkins
- Paper Plates and Bowls
- Plastic Ware
- Candles
- Flashlight
- Scissors
- Batteries

Pantry Items & Staples

- Flour
- Yeast
- Salt and Pepper
- Granulated sugar
- Powdered sugar
- Brown sugar
- Baking powder
- Baking soda

- Corn meal
- Corn starch
- Cocoa
- Vanilla extract
- Cooking oils
- Spices
- Ketchup
- Mustard
- Mayonnaise
- Salad dressing
- Barbeque sauce
- Butter
- Bread
- Milk
- Peanut Butter
- Jelly
- Snack items
- Water
- Coffee
- Tea
- Soda
- Juice

Using Your Home as a Base

"I honestly if I get a vacation I'm gonna go and sit on my couch in New York cause that's the one place I haven't been for a very long time." ~ Matt Damon

When enjoying a staycation, you use your home as a base of operations. Think of places to go and things to do that are a short distance from where you live because for staycation ideas, it's all about location. Where you live is a big factor in deciding where you will go for your day trip and activities. For instance, if you live in the middle of the United States, a beach trip is not something you will plan to do in a day during your staycation. You may however, be able to catch a rodeo nearby – something someone from New York City will not be able to do. And so on.

These next few sections are divided into types of activities separated by the time it takes to do them. You'll find a section on day trips, activities you can do in an afternoon or evening and at home ideas along with some theme days and even an idea just for adults. All have doable tips and useful resources to help make your staycation planning a huge success!

Day Trip Basics

Day trips are outings that your family can comfortably take in a day. You leave your humble abode, go somewhere to do something, spend the day and return home to sleep, using your home as your base of staycation operations instead of a hotel. In this section of the book I will give you tips on planning a day trip and I will give you ten great day trip ideas for your summer staycation. So let's get started!

In order to have a great time during your day trip, you need to plan. That is where some families go wrong – in the planning of their day trips. They do not take into account the travel time, they plan too many activities for the time allotted or they fail to plan at all. When you are on staycation, you don't want to spend too much time traveling, rushing or trying to figure out what you are going to do or how you are going to fit it all in once you get there. After all, part of the point of a staycation is to not have the high costs of travel and a lot of stress.

Pick a place for your family's staycation day trip by offering viable ideas to your family and allowing them to decide – either by vote or consensus. To decide if a day trip spot is a viable idea, ask yourself how long is it going to take to get there? If it will take more than an hour to three hours, you may want to rethink that spot. Perhaps place it in the pile of possible weekend visits in your future. You do not want to spend too much of the day in the car. Either does your spouse and kids. That said I have traveled four hours to a beach for a day trip with my girls. We left very early in the morning and came home late at night. At the time, my daughters were of an age where they slept in the car, so the trip didn't seem as long to them. But, I wouldn't do that unless I really wanted to go to where we were going and we all did, which made it doable for us.

Planning your day trip can seem as problematic as planning your entire staycation. Here are some tips that will help make the planning less time consuming and just easier in general:

- Keep one pocket in your staycation organizer dedicated to each day trip. In it keep your pamphlets, tickets, maps, confirmation numbers and reservation information.
- Make packing a family responsibility. Plan and pack what your family's needs, but allow your kids to be in charge of planning and packing their wants. This will take some of the pressure off as you can keep your focus on the necessities for the trip.
- Get your family's input and ideas at the very beginning of your planning. You don't want to scrap plans you have spent time making because your family would rather do something else. The easiest way to do this is directly after the decision of where you are going is made. Simply ask the question, "What do you want to do there?"

- Plan one less activity than you think your family can do, but save the information just in case. This way, if you really are under-scheduled for the day, you can add back in an activity without much of a hassle than if you are overscheduled and you have to skip something someone in the family was looking forward to doing.
- Keep everyone abreast of how the planning is going by reporting it on your staycation schedule. When some asks, have them check the schedule and you will not have to spend the time explaining it for every family member.
- Get your family's opinion on all of your staycation day trip ideas. Remind them that because these trips are close to home, you won't have to wait until the next full-week staycation to enjoy one or more of them. Keep a list of the day trip ideas your family would like to try throughout the year.
- Add to the excitement of the day trip by building your family's anticipation. Talk about the plans at dinner, share bookmarked websites with your teens via their social networking pages and model your excitement to your kids.

Packing for Day Trips

As George Carlin was always fond of saying, "You gotta have a place for your stuff." During your family's day trips on your staycation, that place goes from being your home to being your car because while you're on your day trip you will need things that you can't carry around the whole time and you won't have a hotel room nearby to store them in.

While this seems semi-problematic, it really isn't. Packing the car with some standard items families need and then the things you'll need for the activity you have chosen will pretty much cover it. I have the standard list below and I mention specific items for the ten day trips in their section. The only other things you will need are those elusive items that would cater to the whim of your children if they ever made it to the car – but they don't. So don't worry about them, I have a plan for you. (You know what I'm talking about: "Mom, I forgot my_____________!" Fill in the blank.)

Here is what you do: Hand each child a backpack that is theirs to use for their day trip activities. Tell them that they are responsible to bring what they want to do or what they feel they need on the trip. And then let them have that responsibility. If your child forgets something, tell them that it is okay, but they will want to try and remember it the next time – keeping the ball in their court.

Day Trip Packing for Babies and Toddlers

- Car seat
- Diaper bag
- Diapers
- Changing pad
- Baby powder and lotion
- Zippered plastic bags
- Wet wipes
- Bathing supplies
- Nursing pads and burp pads
- Bibs
- Baby food and spoon
- Bottles, nipples and caps
- Formula and/or juice
- Pacifiers
- Collapsible stroller with canopy or umbrella
- Front or back child-carrying pack, or sling style
- Blankets
- Large plastic bags for wet clothes
- Medications the baby is using
- Medications in case needed (teething, fever, cold)

Day Trip Packing for School-age Children and Teens

- Backpack or fanny pack
- A change of clothes
- Extra socks
- Jacket and rain gear
- Cell phones
- MP3 Player or iPod

- Any medications your child is taking, along with med alert bracelets

Day Trip Packing for Adults

(Includes standard things for the car)

- Backpack or fanny pack
- A change of clothes
- Extra socks
- Jacket and rain gear
- Cell phones
- Wallet, money, credit cards
- ID or driver's license
- Car and house keys
- Eyeglasses and/or contact lenses - complete with lenses supplies
- Medical insurance cards
- Prescriptions and other medications
- First-aid kit; complete with aloe vera gel, insect repellent, anti-itch cream, tweezers, feminine hygiene items
- Combs and brushes
- Disposable wipes and paper towels
- Trash bags
- Dinner reservation confirmations

Car Trips: Tips for Being on a Long Car Ride

If you are planning a day trip or activity that involves a long car ride you will want to plan a smooth one. Family car rides can sometimes make or break a family activity, so it is important to plan them out in order to get the best possible result. Here are a few tips on how to make your staycation family car trips as best as they possibly can be:

- Be sure everyone is rested when you are on the way to a family activity in the car. If you have been running around all day doing activities, then you can expect the kids to be tired and non-cooperative. It's best to schedule your activities around rest times so that everyone can have an enjoyable time.
- Pack an activity bag for your young children. Or help them do their own. Things to keep little hands busy. Give out the toys slowly, so as to keep your young child's interest.
- Even older children appreciate something new to look at or do at when traveling. We have purchased new game apps for our older kids systems and my sister gets a new children's DVD for her portable player when she travels to see our parents. Got to love technology!
- Have plenty of water and snacks. Non-salty snacks are best in the car to keep the kids from having to drink too much.
- This brings me to the next tip: plan to stop often. If you make a plan of stopping often, you

will not be frustrated when you do have to stop. Remember you are on vacation, no one needs to be anywhere at any particular time. Also, do you have a child who is potty training or has to go immediately? You may want to bring along a portable potty, just in case.

- Let the kids bring a pillow and blankets to cozy up in as much as they possibly can during the trip. Being comfortable when you are traveling is important to them.
- Travel games can be fun for the whole family. Our family has been playing a version of 20 Questions for years. Basically it is all about cartoon characters, classics, Disney and anything that is currently running. We start by trying to guess the cartoon character and end up taking about times when we were kids or laughing at my husband trying to mimic his old-time favorites. These are the simple things that bring families together and make great staycation memories.

Should the Family Pet Stay or Go?

I'll start this section of the book admitting that I am a pet lover. But I am not a lover of the chores that are associated with having a pet. As one of the adults in my household, it falls to me or my husband to either do said chores or make certain they were completed. During our staycation the question becomes, do I want that responsibility when I am taking a vacation at home? Let's take a look at that question by using an example of two different families.

One type of family enjoys having a dog and they love it, but it is not part of their extended family. It does not go everywhere with them nor does it do everything with them. This family would need to find someone to take care of the dog while they went on a day trip. If this is the case and taking care of the dog becomes a hassle during your staycation, my suggestion is to use your kennel services for the duration of the staycation.

The other type of family sees the dog as another person and it literally goes everywhere with their family. You plan around it and only visit places where the dog will be able to come as well. If you take your dog everywhere and that is part of the planning you made for your staycation, then by all means keep him home with you.

As for other family pets that require less work and are able to be home all day while you are on a day trip, like birds or cats, there is no reason to have them boarded or watched as their needs won't impeded your ability to relax during your staycation.

But if you are keeping your family pet home for your staycation, you will need to plan around it. Call to have someone check on or feed it during your day trips. Clean – or get your kids to clean – its cages before your staycation starts as part of the preparation. Make sure there is enough food to feed it throughout the entire staycation so you will not need to go to a store during your week off – check their medications as well.

Remember that a staycation should help you relax and if you do not feel that you will have any 'peace of mind' because you have the responsibilities of the family pets as well as the family, by all means find them a place to go even if the kids object. I give you permission to take a break from the pet chores.

Maximize Your Home Entertainment

Between DVDs, video game systems and games, cable or satellite television, board games, books, etc., families spend a lot of money on home entertainment. Take advantage of this investment you have made during your staycation. Here is how:

Pull out all video games and video game systems. Clean them off and organize them. Do you need new batteries or a memory card? Put it on your list to get before the staycation starts. Then place it in the activities section of the staycation schedule.

Have the entire family find a book that they would like to read. Whether or not they read it all during staycation is not the goal. Just having one available that you want to read will give you something to do if there is a lull and you want to relax with a book. Take your kids to the library and pick up a book if there isn't one in the house for them.

Check the television listings for favorite shows and movies. Mark the time of the shows on your staycation schedule.

Vote on what movies you want in the house for the staycation. Make a list of movies you have that everyone may want to see and take a look at your other alternatives, like Netflix movies if you have a membership. I find a lot of shows for different age groups at the Instant View Movies in Netflix. I mark them for later times and then my kids are able to select one easily off of my list.

Have you played any board games with your family lately? If you have some in your home, dust them off and place them in an area where everyone can see them. That way they are there when you need them.

Look around at your ability for outside activities in your backyard. Games, balls, sandboxes and swings are all full of fun potential. Prepare your outdoor chairs and croquet pieces for use during your staycation.

Video cameras and home movies are also very entertaining if your family enjoys making creative and fun videos. These are also fun to share with extend family that live far away through private channels online.

10 Fun Summer Staycation Day Trips

Summer is just chuck full of fun family activities. So picking a day trip for your staycation is more about weeding through the ideas then coming up with one. Here are ten fun ideas I recommend along with a ton of tips for each.

Go to the Beach

Fun in the sun with the family! A day trip to the beach, relaxing in the sand and playing in the surf may be just what you need during your staycation. One day to soak in the warmth and then you can go home to shower and relax in your own beds instead of dealing with a sandy hotel room. Here are tips on having a fun filled and safe family beach day:

If the beach you are going to has a charge for use, pre-purchase any tags you'll need to avoid long lines when you get there. Sometimes beaches charge a fee for visitors to help offset the costs for lifeguards and clean up fees. To show that you have paid they will issue a plastic tag to wear which often can be mailed to you before you go.

Get a list of the beach rules and plan accordingly. For instance, some beaches will require that shade umbrellas only be placed on the upper half of the beach, not so close to the water. Or, you may not be allowed to walk on the sand dunes or fly a kite in crowded areas.

Choose and area of beach where there is a lifeguard on duty. Not only is this the safest way for a family to enjoy a day at the beach, it will also give you added piece of mind if you have school age children who will go off to swim independently.

Talk to your kids about the ocean swimming. For kids that may be used to swimming in a pool, the ocean with its tide and currents, is very different to swim in. Talk to your kids about this and don't be too quick to allow them to go off on their own. Even with a lifeguard on duty, you want your child to have the basics of ocean swimming down before letting them swim independently.

Check to see if there are public changing facilities. Some beaches do not allow you to change your clothing in their restrooms and they get too crowded. If this is how the beach you are visiting is run, you'll want to be sure everyone has their bathing suits on under their clothing before getting to the beach. One worthwhile purchase for beach day trips when you have a family is a privacy changing room or cabana tent. Even if there are public areas to change in, the privacy tent will prevent standing in long lines with your kids in tow.

Shade tents can also double as a privacy tent on the beach. A shade tent is a useful item when you have young children who will need a nap or may want to be out of the sun for part of the day. One caution for adults if you opt for a shade tent instead of the cabana type: you will have to change sitting down as shade tents are of the pop-up type and aren't made for tall people to stand up in. And even a short adult is considered tall when in one of these tents.

If the beach has a boardwalk with shops, activities and restaurants, make a plan to walk around and check them out. The best time to do this is right after everyone has eaten in order to avoid hungry and bored children in a store. Stores may be a little more crowded at that time, but that is because it's a good time to go. Be sure to grab some information pamphlets for your next beach day trip – or to plan your next 'stay away' vacation.

Don't try out any new foods on your kids (or you) while at the beach. If your child has never had shell fish, this is not the time to test it out. While allergies may be almost non-existent in your family, you really don't want to take that chance on your day trip. If you are planning to go to the beach for your staycation and want to have a seafood meal while there, serve shell fish twice at home before you go to be on the safe side.

Write down your packing list and check it before leaving. When traveling to the beach with your family you are going to have to haul quite a bit of stuff. You'll want to be sure to bring sun screen, towels, water, snacks and an extra change of clothes not to mention personalized stuff that you'll need or the kids will want. If you have older children and teens, let them be in charge of what they want to bring. But have them make a list that you check over first. For younger kids, help them make their own list of what to pack and which play things they want to bring. Here is a sample packing list that you may use:

Clothing and Beach Items

- Swimsuits, one for each person
- Beach towels, one for each person plus two extra
- Beach cover-ups, hats, sandals or flip-flops and sunglasses
- Waterproof sunscreen with the highest SPF for kids; SPF 30 for adults and teens
- Lip balm with sunscreen
- Body lotion for after-sun
- Large beach bag, one for every person
- Cooler to keep water and other cold food items
- Water safety devices for young swimmers, not swimmy toys, check for beach appropriateness
- Folding beach chairs
- Beach umbrella; some beaches rent these
- Large family-size blanket or quilt
- Privacy and/or shade tent

The Fun Stuff

- Books and magazines for kids and adults
- Toys, playing cards, small games

- Buckets, shovels, sifters and sand castle molds
- Frisbee, paddle ball, inflatable beach ball and kites
- Boogie and surf boards
- Camera and film or memory stick
- Zippered plastic bags for collecting shells and sand

Online Resources for Your Beach Day Trip

NRDC Safe Beaches by State
http://www.nrdc.org/water/oceans/ttw/200beaches.asp
Lists popular U.S. beaches and rates them based on various health criteria.

5 Beach Safety Tips for Family Fun
http://www.pediatricsafety.net/2011/06/5-beach-safety-tips-for-family-fun/
While beach outings are one of the highlights of summer, they also present serious hazards – from sunburn and jellyfish stings to riptides and lightning this article gives you tips on how to stay safe.

10 Beach Photography Tips
http://www.digital-photography-school.com/10-beach-photography-tips
Take great pictures if your family day trip at the beach with these tips.

Take a Jaunt to the Country Or City for a Day

When a family lives in an urban or rural area, they find that they would like to get a taste of how the city-fold or country-folk live. They like to see the way the 'other half live' and experience life from their perspective. As both trips have an abundance of things to do and see, I'll split them up to give your some tips for each trip.

If you have never taken the trip to your closest city or meandering countryside, talk to someone who has and ask for any local tips that they have to offer. Plan to go back so that you don't feel the need to fit everything in and relax. Take in all of the positives and show your children how small a world we live in by introducing them to this different area that is so close to where you live.

Tips for taking a trip into the city:

Pick one or two things to see and do and enjoy them. Don't plan to do too many activities or you will miss out on what you are doing. Remember to wear comfortable shoes and that walking around in the city is an experience unto itself – enjoy that as well.

Plan where you are going to go before leaving. Give yourself time to enjoy the things you are planning to do and don't rush. One good thing about this day trip is it is close to home and you can do it again soon if you find that your family wants to.

Find free things to do. Walking tours of parks or historic sites and free admission to rehearsal shows, there are plenty of free things to do in the city if you know where to look. Ask at the visitor's center and take a look on city travel websites.

Map out your path of where you are going before leaving. It is easier to get your family to where they want to go in the city if you know where you want to go. Get a visitors map to the city and take a look at Goggles maps. You may even want to take an online stroll of the area via Google Earth or through the Street Maps program. This way you will be able to recognize the area when you get there. While I feel this step is important one when you are on your own, it is even more important when you are with your kids. You can get easily distracted on the city streets and can get lost. If these extra steps are taken, you can avoid that problem.

Take public transportation into the city. Finding parking in the city is next to impossible or if you know of a garage, it costs a lot of money. Having a car when you are in the city is really more of a hindrance than anything. Leave it at home – or at the train station – and take a bus or train into the city.

Buy tickets for shows or museums prior to your trip into the city. Anytime you can avoid a line, do so. This is probably the best tip I can give to families as waiting is ten times harder to do with kids. Walking in and taking a seat while bypassing a long line at the theaters door is such a good feeling.

Pack as light as possible. You do not want to have to haul a heavy bag around the city all day. You can split the essentials between everyone in the family, allowing even school age children to carry a small bag. Keep important items, like keys, identification and money in a passport wallet that is placed under a shirt or jacket. Even if you are in a safe part of a city, you'll want to take this extra precaution.

Online Resources for Your Visit the City Day Trip

Big Cities Vacations
http://familyfun.go.com/vacations/great-vacations/big-cities-vacations/
Articles from Disney's Family Fun on specific cities to visit.

Kid-friendly City Guides
http://www.deliciousbaby.com/travel/
Offers guide and reader suggestions for many cities, organized by state.

Tips for Taking a Day Trip into the Country

Take the scenic route. You'll love the views, so have your camera ready. Bring books or guides about the area with you so you can share information with your kids about where they are going and what they are seeing.

Map out your road trip as the wide open spaces can lead you astray. While driving the country roads is relaxing, it takes a while to figure out that you've gotten yourself lost. So, check your maps often.

Plan your trip on a day in which the area has a market open. Most famers markets are only open one or two days during the week. Bring a cooler or a hot/cold bag to store your fresh produce purchases.

Plan to stop at a pick-your-own fruit farm. Going to the country when fruit is in season, is one of the best times. If you do plan on doing this, bring a box of quart size zip plastic bags or a large bowl with a lid to store the fruit in for the way home.

Take a tour of a working farm where your kids can feed the chickens and you can get a sampling of some home cooked goods. Carry some hand sanitizer with you wand some baby wipes for quick clean up. Tractor rides at working farms are fun as well. Call ahead to see what is offered and what you will need to pay for as sometimes being on the farm is free, but carriage and tractor rides have a fee.

Eat at a local restaurant and try the dish they are famous for – whatever it is. For instance, if you are in Amish country you should try their Chicken Pot Pie or Pork and Sauerkraut dishes –yum!

Plan your pit stops to be at a place that you want to see. Stop along with way to hike a trail or to take pictures. Be careful of the kids and traffic when stopping along the road. Often there are tourist things you can see and do on your way out to the country. Don't miss those. I recommend you see them on your way instead of one your way home because you may be too tired to stop at that time.

Everyone in the family should wear comfortable footwear that you don't mind getting dirty in farm mud and muck, especially if you will be spending some of the day at a working farm doing some of the work.

Online Resources for Your Visit the Country Day Trip

AMS Farmers' Markets
http://search.ams.usda.gov/farmersmarkets/
AMS works to maintain a current listing of farmers markets throughout the United States.

Visit a State or National Park

State and national parks are full of fun things for families to do. So much so that people write full books about each park. This means, if your family wants to do a day trip to a state or national park, gather as much information as you can and defiantly invest in the guide for that park. There could be valuable information in your state's guide to all parks as well. You can normally find these guides for sale at your local and state visitors' center or at an online bookstore like Amazon.com or BarnesandNoble.com.

State and national parks often have a fee that work a bit differently. For instance, they may charge for a full day per person or per car. Sometimes you have to purchase a seven-day pass, whether you are coming back or not. But all in all, the fee is never astronomical and it does go towards preserving the park, which is a good thing.

Have a family meeting about what activities you would like to do at the park because you will want to know what you will be doing before you get there. This is the only way to know what to pack and how to get ready for your family's day trip as there are many different activities to do.

Take lots of pictures and encourage your children to try new things. For instance, the park may have a ropes course, white water rafting or a horseback riding trail. These new experiences will help your children grow to be well-rounded individuals and they make for very fun family memories.

Teach your children respect for the land we have in our state and national parks. Keep your area clean of litter and try to leave the area in better condition than the way you found it.

About Annual Park Passes

The offers an annual America the Beautiful Pass. Information from their site:

"A pass is your ticket to more than 2,000 federal recreation sites. Each pass covers entrance fees at national parks and national wildlife refuges as well as standard amenity fees at national forests and grasslands, and at lands managed by the Bureau of Land Management and Bureau of Reclamation. A pass covers entrance and standard amenity fees for a driver and all passengers in a personal vehicle at per vehicle fee areas (or up to four adults at sites that charge per person). Children age 15 or under are admitted free."

The pass is currently covers everyone in the car up to 4 adults, so your whole family if you are a family of four or if you children are all under the age of 15-years-old. This is quite a savings if you have a national park close by.

Many state park services offer passes as well. You will need to check with your state parks service for more information on what they offer.

Online Resources for Your Visit to a State or National Park

National Parks Service
http://www.nps.gov
The site is a wealth of information on the U.S. National Parks.

**A listing of state park websites is found in the Appendix.

A Day at the Waterpark

There is nothing more refreshing than a hot summer day spent getting wet and waterlogged at a waterpark. Water parks offer many fun attractions, rides, wave pools, etc. for a family and they all have something to do with getting wet – usually really wet. Hence the 'water' theme - expect to be very wet most of your time there.

Tips for enjoying for your water park adventure:

- Comfortable water shoes are a must. While you can be barefooting it if you chose, sometimes the ground surface is a little rough for little one's feet. I know I have walking on it all day as the bottom of my feet will be sore the next day.
- Bring water bottles to fill at the water fountains. You may not be able to bring water into the park for safety reasons, but you can bring in empty plastic water bottles and purchase water or fill up at the fountains.
- Give your child a chance to get used to the waterpark. While many of the rides are simply slides, some kids may be afraid to try them. Don't push your kids into trying something they don't want to do. Start with easier rides and they may warm up to the idea of the faster more wet ones.
- Using waterproof sunscreen is necessary for everyone in the party, including adults. Invest in the good stuff and slather it on everyone, everywhere. Include the tops of your ears; this

is where I always forget to rub it in. Also, check the timing on the bottle and stick to its recommendations.

- Wear simple suits that will allow you to be active at the park. One piece suits work well as do tankinis, but bikinis often have 'fly-off' accidents on the water rides. Boys should wear suits that they can keep tightened with a drawn string so they don't fall down. Little ones can wear suits with life jackets right in them for added safety.
- Check out the attractions online before going to the park so you will know who is tall enough or old enough for which ride. Make a plan of attack for the park so you spend less time finding seats and figuring out which water rides you want to go on.
- Be prepared to split up for part of the time if you have children of various ages. One will want to go on slides that the other isn't able to because of height or age – or preference.
- Pack towels to keep dry, but not your best ones. Sometimes towels walk away when you set them down. Often, the park will offer towels you can rent. If the water park you are going to visit has this option, take advantage of it.
- Store and lock your valuables. Lockers are made available for a fee at waterparks. Sometimes they take quarters to open and close, sometimes you have to rent the key that opens the locker.

- Bring along your waterproof camera and leave the other one at home. Water and regular cameras do not mix and you do not want to take the chance – a very big chance - of ruining your camera. If you do not have a waterproof camera, considering investing or pick up a disposable one at the waterpark gift shop.
- Someone should wear a waterproof watch. It's easier to stick to a plan of action when you know what time it is. Also, you'll want to be able to check your watch against the 'this how long the line is' times that are posted at popular attractions. If you have kids that are old enough to go off on their own for a bit, you'll want to make sure they have a water proof watch as well.
- Set a meet up time and place if you have kids that will be going off on their own. Be very clear about the times and the exact spot, as spending time looking for your children is never fun. Remind them before they leave to be safe and pay attention to the park rules.
- Bring a small emergency kit. Include Band-Aids, gauze and antiseptic spray. The first aid hut at waterparks can get very busy and you will have to wait in line for simple cuts. Try to avoid the line for a stubbed toe or other small injury.
- Do not wear suits with zippers, buckles or any type of metal. The park will not allow you to go on attractions or in the pools with them. Metal pieces come off and can hurt other people and

the attraction itself. It is especially important to check the suits of your teens. If your teen gives you a hard time, have them bring the other suit with them just in case. But be sure that they do, because there is nothing that kills a good time at a waterpark then a child or a teen that has to sit out.

- Choose the least busy day of the week to go to the park. That is often a Monday or Tuesday, but you can call the park and ask whet their numbers are when you are making your staycation plan with your family. Since you have a week off for your staycation, take advantage of the days when the lines will be short and the park will be less crowded.
- Start checking the weather forecast the week before. Be aware of any rain or thunderstorms that may happen on your waterpark day. If they are in the forecast, switch your staycation days around to place your waterpark visit on one where there will be good weather.
- Come prepared if you have little ones. Use plastic diapers made for swimming and bring extra, just in case. For those that are potty training, this is not the time to practice.
- Bring your own lifejackets. While you can rent them at the park, it is easier to spot your own kids if they are wearing their lifejacket.

Online Resources for Your Day at the Waterpark

Find Water Parks and Indoor Water Park Resorts
http://themeparks.about.com/od/finduswaterparks/u/FindWaterParks.htm
Discover where to get wet with About Theme Park's comprehensive find-a-water park search feature for hundreds of water parks and indoor water park resorts.

WaterParks.com
http://www.waterparks.com
Find a waterpark nearby or at your vacation destination. Interactive map provides all the locations & details.

Amusement Park for Day

Why plan a day trip at an amusement park? Even the name says it – you and your family go to amusement park to be amused, to have fun! The parks are made to be a laugh a minute for families – or gasp in my case. And if they are within an easy driving distance, they make a perfect day trip during your family staycation. Here are some tips to make the most of your day trip:

- Get a guide book or visitor's map and pamphlets for the park you have chosen to go to and do some planning. You'll want everyone to have input as to what they want to see and do. The question I ask each member of my family is: What is the one thing that if we didn't get to it, you would be disappointed in our trip." This gets right to the root of the matter, the one thing they really want to do. Then I take those things and plan each of them in, adding other attractions, breaks, meals in and around them.

- Talk to your family about being safe in the park at least a full week before you depart. Agree on meet up rules for older children who will be allowed to roam and go on attractions on their own. Set up a way to communicate with each other – which shouldn't be too hard to do in this cell phone age.
- Go to bed early the night before. Even though your kids will be very excited the night before the trip, plan quiet time and try and get everyone to bed early. This will ensure a fresh start to your fun day at the park.
- Further your research with an online search about the park. Get ideas from other park goers on online forums and blogs. Pick up tips that are specific to your family. For instance, where does one take a break with a sleepy two-year-old? At Walt Disney World, you take a 15 to 20 minute ride on the railroad and let your little ones rest their eyes.
- Bring the sun screen and use it. Slather that stuff on noses, ears, faces – all over. After you do the kids, get some on yourself too. Sunburn is not the memory you want to take home from this family trip.
- Have lots of water available. If the kids are tired of plain water, go for the Popsicle and Italian ice treats to keep hydrated. Steer clear

of soda and milk based ice cream as they do not hydrate as well.

- Take advantage of special waiting in line rules for parents of small children. Often you can go on a ride while your spouse has the younger children and when the ride is complete your spouse can hop right on instead of having to re-wait in line.
- Allow the older kids some independence. Going to an amusement park during your staycation is an especially useful day trip for families who have children of varying age groups. Allow older kids to bring a friend so they can be independent in the parks and they will be safe with a buddy.
- Count heads often. Pay special close attention to where your kids are walking when going from one attraction to the next. Placing school-aged kids in front of you and holding the hands of your younger children will ensure that you will not lose anyone in your group.
- Enjoy the park through your kids' eyes and get it on camera. Share the wonder and excitement with them – this is the magic of a family fun day trip. Don't forget to take a picture here and there, so everyone will be able to remember what a great time they had.
- Remember that this day trip is part of your staycation – relax! You don't have to see everything that is offered, especially since you can schedule this trip again as you are close to home.

- Eat a breakfast bar on the way to the park, plan a brunch there and make reservations for an early dinner. If you eat a meal at the park at 10 a.m. and 3 p.m., then you can grab a snack at noon and 7 p.m. You and the kids will be feed and not be hungry. But most importantly, you will miss the mealtime crowds and have less in-line-waiting time for the theme park attractions when everyone else is seeking out their meals.
- Buy large snacks and split them. The prices for a large snack are often not much more than the smaller size. It can save you a little by sharing the snack with your little one, plus, you'll waste less.
- Waiting in line is part of being at an amusement park, but it doesn't have to be a bore. Play a simple game with your kids - like I-Spy or Park Themed 20 Questions – while you wait. Also, check options for lines when you research the park. There may be ways to avoid a long line, like the Fast Pass option given at Walt Disney World.
- If you have younger children with short little legs, take advantage of stroller rentals or bring your own. Even if your child has grown out of a stroller for other outings, it is good to have one at an amusement park as their legs will get tired and they will want to sit and relax. Most parks have stroller parking at children's attractions – just be sure not to leave your valuables unattended with the stroller.

- You'll want to plan your amusement park day before a day at home in which you've scheduled ample time of rest and relaxation. Plan a morning of sleeping in with continental breakfast that the kids can get on their own while you catch some extra Zzzzzs. While the fun is worthwhile, you will be tired so plan for it and the rest of your staycation will go smoothly.
- Consider going back. If you find your family really enjoyed their time at the park, you may want to consider an annual pass to the park. Check the prices and crunch the numbers, then take a look at your annual calendar to see if you can make it work.

Online Resources for Your Day at the Amusement Park

Find Theme Parks and Amusement Parks
http://themeparks.about.com/od/findusthemeparks/u/FindThemeParks.htm
Search for Disney, Universal, Six Flags, and other theme parks and amusement parks, including park profiles, reviews, vacation-planning advice, and other park information.

Tips for Taking Amusement Park Vacations Planning
http://travel.kaboose.com/theme-parks/amusement-park-vacations.html
Use these tips and advice on how to make your trip as easy and carefree as possible.

Go White Water Rafting or River Tubing

Have a river nearby that you would like to meander down or would you and your family prefer to ride the white water instead? Local rivers can provide exciting fun for today's staycationing family. The perfect rafting or tubing trip is a combination of fun, adventure and safety. Here are some tips to make this family day trip as prefect as possible:

- Go with a group that is led by a certified guide who is CPR and First Aid Trained for adults and children. The guide will be in their own boat; unless you want one in your boat then you can get one for a fee. From there they will guide the group and help where needed. Yes, white water rafting trips are risky, but statistically you are safer in a white water craft, if you are using all of the safety precautions, then you are in a car.
- Fit the trip to your family dynamics. Many white water rafting companies have trips for young children. Do not push a young child or inexpericnced person to take a trip that is for intermediate rafters. Even if you are experienced rafters, you'll want to go at an easier pace with your kids until they become experienced or you risk scaring them into not wanting to ever go again or getting them hurt.
- Bring a disposable water proof camera to take shots of your family's white water rafting adventure. Leave your expensive camera at

home or on shore. On trips that involve so much water, there is no need to risk your expensive equipment.

- Note that you will get wet on white water rafting and tubing trips. There is really no way to stay dry. You may even fall out of the boat once or twice... it's all a part of the fun.
- Tubing trips tend to be more relaxing and last about 2.5 to 3 hours long. You float along the river from one spot to the next splashing, having water fights and checking out the scenery. There will be soft rapids on your trip, which makes it that much more fun.
- When you are tubing, each person has their own tube. Therefore, tubing is best for families with older kids. Many companies will require a certain weight in order to be able to go on the river in their boats; usually around 40 lbs. Weight your kids and ask the company if they are at the appropriate weight before you book a trip.
- Bring enough adults for you size group when white water rafting. You will need to have a responsible adult in each raft or with each group of tubers. Normally, a responsible adult does not include your 18-year-old son unless it is just him and his friends in a raft.
- Ask about water temperature. Even though it is summer, river water can be cold especially for children. Ask what the water temp runs normally on the date of your trip. Wet suits can offset the cold of the water if need be.

Must haves for your white water rafting day trip:

- Life vests and wet suits of cold temperatures
- Sun screen
- Lip balm with sun screen
- Insect repellent
- Motion sickness medication

*For the best online resources for canoeing and boating, check the state and national parks websites listed under the Visit a State or National Park.

Go Canoeing, Boating or Sailing

I know a family who takes their boat to a nearby lake and passes time traversing back and forth from one end of the lake to the other, sometimes allowing the boat to just float along. They'll eat a packed lunch, fish, listen to music and talk with each other. It makes one of those steadfast family days that they will remember forever. If you have a boat, why not take advantage of this type of activity during your staycation? You can plan a family adventure on the high seas or in a nearby lake.

For a boating day trip you will need to plan where to put your boat in the water, plan the day's events – will you fish or are you boating to a destination – and figure out all of the details. Here are some tips that will help:

- Assign boating duties to everyone in the family so that everyone has a part in the chores and safety of your family boating trip. Make a list of what needs to be done and place a name next to each chore. Before leaving land, check each item on the list to be sure it has been done.

- Pack your family for the weather and be prepared with extra clothing, rain gear, hats, etc. in case someone gets wet or if the weather changes. Give each child their own backpack with their things.
- Pack food and water in a cooler for a large boat and canoe. Make small packs of other things to help with using all of the space available on your boat, like under seats. Have your emergency pack where everyone can see it.
- Keep children hydrated as they can dehydrate very easily in the hot sun.
- Water shoes are a must when you go boating and canoeing. Everyone will also need a pair of dry shoes and socks for any walking or hiking at the stops you make.
- Boating in the ocean is a magnificent experience for a family. If you own a sea-faring boat, plan a trip to see dolphins or whales or to catch some crabs.
- If you don't have a boat, sign up with an experienced boating company to take your family out on an excursion. Ask them what they provide and what they suggest you bring. We have enjoyed trips out to the ocean to see dolphins with a group where they provided life vests for even the youngest boaters. But then, I went crabbing with a group that preferred you brought your own life vests for toddlers. Be

sure to research the company against others in the area, try and find the best deal for your family.

- When you go boating, unlike rafting, you should plan on getting too wet – unless you want to. Cameras should be brought on boating trips – you need to remember these fun times – but please take precautions not to get them wet. Either bring along a water-proof camera or place your camera in a water-proof bag.
- Keep the kids comfortable and happy. While we enjoy the relaxation of floating along the water, kids may get bored. Pack a kids' bag with treats, toys, activity books and other fun diversions. Have a small bucket of rocks that they can use to skim in the water. Along the same lines, be sure your kids are comfortable where they are sitting. You can purchase low sitting kids beach chairs for inside a canoe or give them a seat with a backrest in a recreational boat.
- Taking a canoe trip on a lake or river requires two people to paddle each canoe. Both should be healthy and strong enough to do this job, or you may get stuck on the other side of the lake.
- Life vests are a must-have. As the parents of any family who boats knows, life vests are very important to take on a boating trip. But also, for children, you will need to test their life vests as this is a good practice to help the kids feel more comfortable about how their life vest works and for you to know that their personal

flotation device or PFD works for them. Pre-boating trip, take your kids to a pool or lake, put the life vest on correctly and let them get in the water. Feel free to let them play in their life vests until they feel more at ease with its use. Teens may feel they do not need to use a life vest, or they will put it on but not use it correctly. It bothers them, makes them feel like a little kid, they know how to swim, it isn't comfortable, etc. Explain to your teen that it is important to wear a life vest as you can't swim if you get knocked out. Wear a PFD yourself and model appropriate behavior. It may help to give your teen the choice of what type of PFD they would like to wear.

- Check in with the visitors' center. Talk to the visitor center for the water area you will be boating on and have them check to see if there is a planned boating or canoe trip or map that takes you to different parts of the local area. It's always nice to know where you can stop your canoe or sailboat to have a campfire or enjoy a short hike.
- If you are going out to the wilderness for your boating trip, sign in at the closest ranger's station. Check to see if there are any rules or special circumstances in the waters you wish to traverse, like down trees or fast running water because of recent rainfall.
- If you are taking fishing trip out in the ocean, see if you can't eat your catch when you get back. Some companies that take fishing trips

out will prepare your catch as a meal which is a very fun experience – and yummy too.

- Create a family sea ditty, even if you are just on a river. A silly song about your family being on the water creates memories that will never be forgotten – especially if you are like me and you can't sing.

Must haves for your boating or canoe day trip:

- Life vests
- Sun screen
- Lip balm with sun screen
- Hats or sun visors
- Insect repellent
- Motion sickness medication
- Maps

*For the best online resources for canoeing and boating, check the state and national parks websites listed under the Visit a Park Day Trip.

Shopping Spree Day Trip

Planning a shopping spree for a staycation day is fun for many, maybe not all. Generally, women like to shop and men do not. So this may be a staycation day where the men and women go their separate ways and do their own thing. Nothing wrong with that! One of the positives of being on a staycation is how easy it is to have a flexible schedule with your whole family. If you would like to have a shopping spree day, by all means, suggest it to your family and plan it.

Here are some tips on having a successful shopping spree day:

- Make it count. A shopping spree can be a very useful type of staycation day, if say it's the end of the summer and you need to get your children their school clothes. Or you have a wedding to attend and you would like to purchase a new dress for yourself. Take a look at the family calendar and plan your purchases accordingly.
- Sign up for flyers and notifications at your favorite stores. Check these for sales and events during your staycation. Also, look for sales and discounts on certain brands at their company website or email newsletter.
- Get ideas from everyone in your group about what stores they would like to visit. Try to fit in at least one idea from each person in the group so that everyone has a good time. Write out a plan of which stores you would like to do you're shopping in. Combine stores that are close together to condense your drive time.
- Suggest a baby watching trade-off to your spouse. If you have young children and having a shopping spree will mean dragging the baby –and all of their stuff – along isn't your idea of a good time, this is a viable option. You'll take the baby for an afternoon so he can do something he wants, and then he can take a turn watching the baby. Or, call your regular

sitter and leave the kids at home – another staycation benefit!

- Meet your family for a meal. Plan a lunch or dinner at an eatery where the entire family enjoys eating, but is not one that you eat at often. Then, plan to meet there and enjoy a meal together. Also, plan a restful evening after an all-day shopping spree trip.
- Sign up for a class or demonstration. Craft stores and specialty shops offer classes and demonstrations of their products. My daughter took a cooking class in a specialty kitchenware shop that offered them to the public through their newsletter and I enjoy a card making class at my local scrapbook store.
- Get away from your normal stomping grounds and hit the outlets or the bigger mall 'two towns over'. Being someplace new or to a store that you wouldn't normally shop at makes it all the more exciting. Keeping it close to home – staycation style – doesn't take away from the excitement.
- Dress for success. If you are going on a shopping spree with teen girls and they like to get dressed up when they go out shopping. Anticipation and getting ready is part of the fun! But, you will want to remind everyone to wear comfortable walking shoes as they will be on their feet much of the day. You may also want to wear an undershirt so you can try on jackets and sweaters without carting them to the dressing room.

- Create a general list of stores you would like to shop, but allow yourself to take some time to browse and window shop as well. Add a few stores that you aren't able to shop in often and go in to browse or pick up something that you really like 'just because'. It's fun to get some new things during vacation – why not still indulge when you are on your staycation?
- Note the time the stores you have on your list are opening and closing. Some specialty shops have different hours and days where they may be closed. Start your shopping spree when the stores open for fewer crowds.
- Curb impulse buying for the whole family. Purchase some gift certificates to give to your kids and tell them that is their spending limit. Kids like using their own cards to purchase things and you can be sure they aren't spending too much money.
- If you are taking your kids on your shopping spree, stop at the play center. Kids need to dispense their energy and a play center is just the ticket to do so. Many malls have play centers right in their food court areas where you can take a break while your kids get to play.
- Create a budget for big purchases. Need to purchase certain items during your shopping trip? Be sure to set the budget amount for the item and stand firm on the price. While you may have to go to a few more stores and haggle a bit with the sales team, getting the price you

need is important enough to walk away from the sale.

- ◈ Plan a special activity during your shopping spree. Enjoy a make-over or get a massage. Adding things you wouldn't normally do will turn your shopping trip into a fantastic staycation shopping spree!
- ◈ Take advantage of the coffee shops and rest areas. Enjoy good conversation with those who are with you over a latte or herbal tea. Drop off packages as you go instead of lugging your purchases around.
- ◈ Bring a pen and receipt holder in your purse. Keep all of your receipts from your shopping spree trip in one place and mark them according to what they are and who they are for if it is not clearly written on the receipt. Another benefit of being on staycation is you will be able to return an item easily if you find it doesn't suit your needs.

Shopping sprees are a perfect activity for staycations with extended family. A shopping spree day is a perfect time to catch up with the women you are related to. It puts everyone on the same level, no one has to serve or host the rest of the group, it gives you something to do if someone is getting on your nerves and everyone can find something they like. It can be a real stress-less outing.

Online Resources for Your Shopping Spree

List of shopping malls in the United States
http://en.wikipedia.org/wiki/List_of_shopping_malls_in_the_United_States
From Wikipedia, the free encyclopedia.

Spend a Day at a Museum

Visiting a museum is an enriching experience for the whole family as museums offer a look into a world that we may never have had the opportunity to see. Museums come in all shapes and sizes, much like families. Many are very large. So large in fact, it would take you several days to get through the whole thing. Like the Smithsonian museums in Washington, DC. Touring and appreciating them takes time. So, if you have a museum like this in your area, plan a full day trip to enjoy it. Here are some tips:

- Gather your information on the museum you will be visiting. To get the most out of a museum visit, get as much information about the exhibits as possible and share them with your family before you go. Virtually visit the museum with your kids.
- Buy advance tickets if you can as they are often discounted and you will save time not having to stand in line. Also, call ahead and see if they have a time when visiting the museum is free.
- Check out the museum online and note the opening and closing times. You may want to be there at opening and take advantage of the

smaller crowds to see the exhibits. You will also want to note if you need to make a reservation for a tour. If so, do this as soon as you know when you will be going because that is a sure sign that they will fill up.

- Make a game of it! Download pictures of the exhibits and art and turn them into flash cards. Give each family member one or two cards and have them try to find the exhibits when you get there. Or create a scavenger hunt check list for your family members to check off the objects as they find them.
- Dress comfortably. While museums are indoors, you'll want to dress with comfortable shoes and layers so no one is too cool or too hot. Sometimes they keep places like museums cool so the exhibits don't get too warm, so bring a jacket.
- Allow each member to pick an exhibit that they absolutely must see. Then go to see each one starting with the pick from the youngest member of the family working your way up to the oldest member of the family. This way no one will be disappointed because you have run out of time to see their favorite exhibit.
- Check out the private and group tours offered at the museum. You may find a family-friendly tour that will take the responsibility of reading all of the exhibits information to your kids. If the museum is close to your home, you may want to check to see if they have kids' camps or

youth clubs that your kids or teens may be interested in.

- Take advantage of rest areas and enjoy a lot of little breaks. While you may not be tired of walking, your children may be. If you break before they get tired, the will stay energetic and excited about the museum visit.
- Much like the television and the internet there are things in a museum that are not for the eyes of children. While nudes immediately come to mind, there are many other exhibits that could be disturbing for young children. I know Bodies: The Exhibition, which I had gotten a chance to see in Las Vegas, is something I would not have shared with my daughters until they were older. Use your best parenting judgment.
- Talk to your kids about the exhibits they will see. For instance, if you will be visiting a space museum, read stories about astronauts and watch a video online about the first space landing on the moon. This will add to their excitement ten-fold.
- Check out your travel to the museum options. If the museum you are planning to visit is in the city, take public transportation instead of driving your car. Parking can be very difficult. If you do drive, call ahead and ask where the best place to park is located – they may have a garage discount.
- Special considerations for your child need to be well thought-out. Children under the age of 12-

years-old should be accompanied by an adult and should never be left alone. And while I've never condoned leashing children, I have a daughter who used to disappear in the blink of an eye. I had to hold her hand everywhere! Do what you need to do to keep your kids with you and safe as museums can get very crowded and you can lose sight of your children very easily. If you are taking a small child or baby into the museum, you should call ahead and see what is allowed to be carried in and if you have to rent a stroller there or use a back pack.

- Check out the museums website. Many museums offer online newsletters that have hours of operation for the month, discounts and news on special activities and exhibits. Sign up right away. Even if you don't make it this time around, you live close enough that you can go another time. Staycations are awesome in that way!

Online Resources for Your Day at the Museum

USA Museums Database

http://museumca.org/usa/

Huge database organized by state or type of museum.

Treasure Hunting Adventures

Many areas in the United States offer treasure hunting fun where families can hike, pan and search for gems, gold or fossils. Kids love the discovery so much they hardly notice that they are learning something as well. Add that you are enjoying a great experience with family and you have an A+ staycation idea. Here are tips on having a fun filled and safe treasure hunting day:

- Nearby colleges may have a dig, call to find out. If there is a fossil dig or gem hunt at a nearby university that allows visitors and gives tours, your local visitors' center is the best place to gain that information or you can call the college and talk to the professor in charge.
- Treasure hunting is hard work – work being the operative word. This type of day trip is for kids who are old enough to walk on their own and have some basic skills - like how to hold a pick axe. If you still have little ones, save this idea for when they have grown up a bit.
- Treasure is usually found out in the dirt, so dress accordingly. Hiking boots, good socks, hats and in layers is your best bet. Rain gear is a must.
- Inquire about equipment before leaving for your trip. Normally it is part of the fee if you are going to an organized dig tour. But if you are visiting a college dig, you may have to bring your own.

- Don't forget the camera. Whichever treasure you decide to go after, bring your camera to document the event and you'll have family memories that are better than any gems or gold. Take pictures of the before, during and after finding the treasure and keep a journal as you go.
- Learn with the class. If the fossil or gem dig is being run by a local college, see if you can get your hands on any information about the dig prior to visiting. Often professors publish a handbook with important information about the dig for their students, which you can purchase at the college bookstore.
- Treasures can also be found along beaches. Sea glass, shark's teeth and beautiful shells are among the fun things you can collect on a beach day trip.

Gold Prospecting 101
http://www.operationgold.com/gold-prospecting/
This site is a definitive resource to gold prospecting, where you'll get a brief overview of the different prospecting techniques and links to gold prospecting articles.

Gold Panning Vacation
http://www.goldfeverprospecting.com/gopava.html
In addition to some of the great gold panning spots listed above, here is a site that provides some good information for planning a gold panning for gold prospecting vacation.

Gold Prospecting, Gold Panning - Places to Find Gold
http://www.49ermike.com/goldloc.shtml
This site has good information about where you can find gold in the United States. Information is organized by state and then by county. These are for 'on your own' type trips.

Top 10 Treasure-Hunting Hot Spots
http://www.travelchannel.com/interests/great-american-vacations/articles/top-10-treasure-hunting-hot-spots
The United States is home to a wealth of treasure hunting possibilities. From gemstones to meteors, discover Travel Channel's picks for America's top 10 treasure hunting hotspots.

Virtual Dinosaur Dig - National Museum of Natural History
http://paleobiology.si.edu/dinosaurs/interactives/dig/dinodig.html
Let your kids dig up this virtual dinosaur and see what happens to it once it goes to the museum.

Gorp.com
http://www.gorp.com
This site offers all types of local information on a variety of outdoor activities, including archaeology.

Fun Activities for an Afternoon or Evening

Home is where the vacation is when you are staycationing, but don't sit in the house too long or you'll suffer from cabin fever and the kids will get bored. Think of your home as your base of operations and get out and do fun activities together.

Hike a Rail Trail or Local Trail

Hiking local trails and rail trails in the United States is a free activity that families enjoy doing every day. Often they lead to areas where you can set up a picnic or see some local history - sometimes both!

The visitor's center in your area will have the information you are looking for about the local trails. They may even have information from your state Audubon Society, and you can turn your family hike into a fun bird watching experience. Taking the time and categorizing the trees that are on the trail or getting pictures of the local wildlife is also fun and educational.

More tips:

- Be sure to bring a Frisbee or ball to play with if you will be stopping to picnic or hang out. Tree and rock climbing are fun outdoor activities you and your kids can enjoy.
- Have a scavenger hunt. Give your family a list of things to find on your hike. You can just

point them out or take digital photos of them to put together in a digital family album of your staycation.

- Make some nature texture art by bringing some white copy paper and crayons. Then do rubbings of the different textures you find on tree barks and stones or large rocks. Mat and frame the artwork then place it on a wall in the family room for a fun memento.

Resources:

Information on local trails can be found at http://www.localhikes.com and http://www.americantrails.org American Trails also offers a magazine you can order on their site.

DayHiker.com
http://www.dayhiker.com
While the site is dedicated to 'extreme' day hikes, it offers tips for hiking that your family can use.

Gorp.com
http://www.gorp.com
This site offers all types of local information on a variety of outdoor activities, including hiking.

Horseback Riding

If you haven't taken your family horseback riding before you are in for a treat. Kids and teens love to watch, pet and ride on horses.

Many local horse farms offer horseback riding to the public. You will be able to find their information at your local visitor's center. You will need to call and set up a time letting them know how many people are in your family that will be riding. There are also farms that will take your family on a private tour and give your private lessons or a family horseback ride for a day. Ask around to friends who have horseback riding lessons and give their teacher's a call.

Resources on horseback riding activities:

HorseandTravel.com
http://www.horseandtravel.com/
Directory of horse trails, riding stables, dude ranches and just about anything else you want to know about a riding a horse.

Horseback Riding Directory
http://horseback-riding.regionaldirectory.us/
The site includes horseback riding service provider pages for every State in the USA plus Washington, DC.

Spend the Afternoon at a Pool (Away from Your Home)

Does your town or club have a pool available for your use? If so, make use of it for an afternoon during your staycation. I was lucky enough to have a pool right down the street from where I lived when my kids were younger. We would walk down to the pool and spend a whole afternoon and my husband would meet us there at dinner time after work. I know of one family who would spend many of their vacation days just hanging out at the pool with friends – they really enjoyed it and I'm sure you will too.

- Call ahead and see which pizza or take-out joint will deliver and enjoy your diner by the pool instead of packing up to come home too soon.
- Even if you can't get there for formal lessons for the kids, maybe you can hire a high school student to teach your child when you can get there.
- Sign up for a class.
- Take advantage of special nights like movie nights at the pool.
- Town and group owned pools provide perfect activities for school age kids and teens during a staycation because they come complete with your child's friends who also have a membership to the pool. This will give you time to relax, read, peruse the magazines that have been stacking up or simply just to sunbath.
- For those with smaller children, group pools offer baby pools in which you can enjoy playing with your little one in the water.
- Some town and group-owned pools have a food stand available as well. If this is so, lighten the load of things you bring from home and purchase snacks or a light meal there.

Pick Your Own Fruit Farms

Are you setting the dates for your staycation during the harvest time of a family's favorite fruit? Great! This is a wonderful activity for your staycation. Picking fruit is not as hard as it sounds and you will get a bountiful harvest to freeze or can that you can enjoy the entire year. Or you can just go pick what you want to eat within the next week or so.

For those picking and freezing or canning for the first time, know that it will take you most of the day, if not into the evening. You'll want to get an early start and have all of the supplies purchased before your staycation. Get everyone involved in the cleaning and preserving. Then be sure to take some out at Thanksgiving for the whole family to enjoy the memory.

In the fall of every year there are many pumpkin patches that offer family activities like a corn maze or a hayride. In our area they even had some carnival rides to enjoy. At a pumpkin patch you can enjoy what activities are offered and then go pick your own pumpkins to decorate your home for the autumn season. This is a great afternoon activity for families who take a fall staycation.

Resources:

Pick Your Own
http://pickyourown.org
List of farms that offer pick your own fruits.

Backyard Camping

Camping in one's own backyard is great fun and comes with all of the amenities. While it is an overnight, it technically is still at your home. You get to sleep in a tent in the backyard with running water only a few feet away – that is my kind of camping!

Backyard camping has actually become a craze in recent years, with a Great American Backyard Campout weekend celebrated annually in June. For more information, check out the site at http://www.nwf.org/Get-Outside/Great-American-Backyard-Campout.aspx

More tips:

- Have the ability to have a campfire; whether you have a fire pit in your backyard or you have to purchase one, it's a good idea to have if you are camping out. Safety first: Don't set up your tent too close to the fire. Also, be sure the fire is out and dosed with water before you go to sleep.
- Bring a book of campfire stories, stories and games to share with your family.
- Do not forget the supplies to roast marshmallows and make s'mores.
- Live in the big city with no backyard? Pop up a pup tent in the family or living room. Light a pine scented candle and make microwave s'mores.

- Allow your kids to take a flashlight and their book to bed with them. Reading in a sleeping bag with a flashlight is a great memory that all kids should share.
- If you have or can borrow a telescope, your family can enjoy star gazing.

Take the Family on Cycling Trip

Does everyone have a bike in your family? Put them to good use by going cycling for the day. Here are some tips:

- Get a map of local bike trails at your local visitor's center.
- If the whole family can bike to the trail safely without driving, great! If not, invest in a bike rack for your vehicle and make this a monthly family activity.
- Don't bite off more than anyone can chew. This is supposed to be a fun family experience. Try not to push anyone's stamina, just enjoy each other while biking. Go at your kids pace instead of them trying to keep up with you. Let them know you will slow down; they just need to ask you.
- Take a break to drink water often.
- Bike to where you can have a picnic lunch or dinner. This may take some planning, like how you will get the meal there. Maybe that is where you can park your car? Or each person can carry a piece of the meal in their backpacks.

- Plan this day by checking that everyone has working equipment and it all fits. Check your child's helmets and be sure they are still the right size for their heads. Check each bike for the tires and the brakes. This should be done a week or more before the staycation so that you will be able to have the bikes fixed if need be.

**Trail resources can be found under Hiking.*

Enjoy Lunch and a Matinee

Is there a sandwich shop your family would enjoy or just a fast food place that your kids don't get to eat at too often? Staycations are perfect for these places. Go, have a meal. Then after you eat, you can see a local matinee at the movie theater or live theater if your area has that available.

If there is a movie out your whole family can enjoy, what not take advantage of the matinee price? Going to a movie in the middle of the day during the week is very vacation-y. Doing so in your own hometown is very staycation-y. Call first for times.

If you have live performances available to you and your family in your local area, by all means take advantage of them during your staycation.

You'll want to plan and early lunch so that you will be ready for the show. Lunch service can sometimes be unpredictably slow as the business crowd fills the restaurants, so plan ahead. If you get done early, you can window shop or just take a walk through your town.

Visit a Science Center

Science centers are hands on science museums that have thrilling exhibits for kids of all ages. Kids love the touching and doing aspect of a science center, even if it is educational. The visit will take up most of a morning or afternoon and can lead to another activity as many centers offer IMAX film tickets or passes to another museum as a package.

Hands on exhibits will teach about technology or electricity in a safe environment. Experiences entice children to do things that they wouldn't think to do on their own. Many a scientist will trace back the first time they loved science to being a time when they saw a fantastic experiment. While schools do their best, science centers have better funding and can offer so much more. They will offer your kids experiences that can affect their future.

Special exhibits keep things new and interesting. If you've already been to your area's science center within the last year, check to see if they are offering new traveling exhibits which tend to switch in and out of science centers every two to three months. Most centers have an area that they devote to a traveling exhibit that goes all over the country. For example, the last time I was at my area's science center they had Egyptian mummies and artifacts from the pyramids. Because they had this traveling exhibit, they created more hands on exhibits about hieroglyphics and mummification. Currently they are offering a 'Tornado Alley 3D Storm' exhibit with hands on interactive weather stations. When I take my kids this time, they will enjoy their favorite exhibits again plus enjoy the new weather exhibits.

Resources:

Association of Science - Technology Centers
http://astc.org/sciencecenters/find.php
Find a science center in your area.

Visit an Aquarium

Aquariums house some of the most beautiful animals of the world that we would never be able to see without them. Kids walk around looking at everything when they visit and it is as wonderful watching their reactions to the fish as it is seeing them yourself. My youngest daughter is enamored with large sea turtles. She loves them because of a trip we made into Boston and our visit to the Aquarium located there. The one tank is about three stories tall and you look in while walking up or down a spiral walkway. She followed the big turtle up and down the tank – many times! Besides having the time of my life watching her not be able to take her eyes off of this creature, I got my exercise.

There is an amazing amount of information around the tanks and throughout the aquarium. Take any pamphlets you can along home to read with the kids and spend some time reading aloud to them as you go. Then point things out in the tank that they may not otherwise see.

Be sure to stop in at the tanks where you can touch things. There will be a well-marked area with attendants where kids – and adults – can touch star fish and other sea life.

Plan your meals around going to the aquarium as the cafeteria is expensive and not overly family friendly. Most aquariums have cafeterias where the food is fast-food type. They are also very crowded at meal time and you will have a hard time finding a seat.

Resources can be found under Visit a Zoo.

Go to the IMAX Theater

The IMAX Theater is an amazing movie-going experience. Its movies are 3D and often made for IMAX alone. Here are some family-friendly tips:

- The swooping imagery and loud surround sound can be overwhelming for young kids under 5-years-old, so be forewarned.
- IMAX can take you to never imagined frontiers of entertainment and places. If you are going to an IMAX movie as part of a science center you will love the detail given in these.
- Many of today's popular motion picture films are being released in 3D and using the technology that the IMAX theaters have to show their films to the public, for instance the

last two Harry Potter films were released in IMAX as well as in regular theaters. Stop in and get a schedule.

- Make sure you get there on time as late seating is not permitted in an IMAX theater for safety issues.
- Sit as close to the center of the screen as you can for the best possible IMAX experience.

Visit a Local Observatory and Planetarium

Observing the sky is a phenomenal experience that everyone in the family will enjoy. If there is an observatory and planetarium in your local area – check your local university if you don't have a public one – than try to place it on your short list of things for your family to do on your staycation. Often they offer shows of sights that have been seen before and many offer public sky watching for free any evening that they are open.

Call ahead and see if there is a gift shop that has books on the topics covered in the show that you can add to your family library. You can entice children to read by extending their experiences through books about what they have seen – and get them excited for another visit.

A visit to an observatory can bring about an interest in space and science in your kids. If you think this is happening with your child, you may want to invest in a telescope that they can use at home to kindle the interest in their new star-gazing hobby.

Factory Tours

Is there a candy or pretzel factory in your area? Do they give tours to the public? Give them a call and find out what time you can tour the factor and if they have any other activities for families. I have enjoyed tours of many types of food companies including pretzels, potato chips, chocolate and others. They always end their tours with a small sample and dropping you off in a store where they sell their wares. This is perfect for a staycation because you can pick up a snack for home along with enjoying the tour!

If you happen to live in an area where there is a popular brand of food or beverage, there is most likely a tour to be seen, but you will have to call for times. Same is true for manufacturing of things like airplanes, cars or motorcycles. And one of the best things about these tours – they tend to be free!

Note to parents of children with food allergies: call ahead and make sure your child will not end up having a reaction to any of the foods used at the factory.

Resources:

Factory Tours USA
http://www.factorytoursusa.com
Comprehensive resource for finding factory tour information for tours available to the public.

Go to the Zoo

Zoos are wondrous places where animals live and do the things animals do and we get to see them doing it. Kids love zoos and so do Moms and Dads. Everything about a zoo is fun; even the stinky reptile house gets a giggle from the kids because of its awful smell. Here are some tips on taking your kids to the zoo:

- Talk to your kids about safety: Animals cannot be fed, Okapis do not make good pets, do not put your fingers in the cages, etc.
- Call ahead and get the zoo's feeding schedule so you can be there to see some of the animals get feed – you may even be allowed to help.
- You'll want to visit a zoo in the morning when the animals are the most active. By afternoon they have slowed down and often are asleep which can be boring for the kids.
- Does your child have a favorite animal? Many zoos offer behind the scenes tour and experiences. Go a step further and call ahead and see if you can sign your family up for one of these.
- Visit the information booth when you arrive at the zoo and get a map and a listing of presentations that will be happening during your visit. Presentations are often free and very informative. Many zoos have visiting animals and they like to show them off or they have a special exhibit that they present to the public.

- Quirky animals make for a great photo album and bedroom art. Let your kids be in charge of a digital camera and create a photo montage of zoo animals for their room.

Resources:

Wikipedia: Okapi
http://en.wikipedia.org/wiki/Okapi

Association of Zoos and Aquariums
http://www.aza.org/
Founded in 1924, the Association of Zoos and Aquariums (AZA) is a nonprofit organization that accredits zoos and aquariums.

Picnic at the Park

Many communities have beautiful parks with recreational facilities that include things like swing sets, ball courts and fields, skate board park, benches and picnic tables, amphitheaters, nature and fitness walks and more. If your community has a park like this, make use of it during your staycation. Here are some tips:

- Call or stop by your community center and pick up a schedule of events in the park. Many times there will be special movies or music nights offered throughout the summer months.

- Bring a basketball, soccer ball and Frisbee, and then let your kids decide what to play with when you get there.
- You don't have to do all of the work for a full-fledged picnic. Pick up a takeout meal – call it in to your local sandwich shop and you are done – and have it at the park instead of at home.
- Make clean up easy by placing all of the trash in the middle of the disposable table cloth, Wrapping it up and placing it in the trash bag. Then deposit the trash bag in the park dumpster.
- You may have to reserve a picnic table by calling beforehand if your park is a busy one. Or you can go and if there is one available – great! If not, spread your tablecloth out on the grass.
- Don't forget to bring a first aid kit in case of small mishaps.

Check List of Things You Need for a Picnic at the Park

- Table cloth (disposable)
- Paper plates
- Plastic utensils
- Plastic cups
- Trash bag
- Hand wipes and Paper Towels
- Food and drink
- Outside toys, balls
- Blankets and chairs to sit on

Resources:

NRPA
http://www.nrpa.org
Their mission is to advance parks, recreation, and environmental conservation efforts that enhance the quality of life for all people.

City Parks Blog
http://cityparksblog.org/
A joint effort of the Center for City Park Excellence at the Trust for Public Land and the City Parks Alliance to chronicle the news and issues of the urban park movement.

Go Bowling

Bowling is a family game that is kid-friendly and can be enjoyed anyone of any age. Most bowling alleys have items that help even young children bowl. Here are some tips on taking your family bowling during your staycation:

- Bowlers of all ability levels can bowl a game together. You do not need to have a special place for those in the family who have never bowled before. One lane can have bumpers and the other can be open, if need be.
- You do not have to bring special equipment to the bowling alley – just don't let anyone forget their socks. Everything you need to use is already there.

- If you ask nicely, you can probably get a tour of the back of the alley and see the pins get set up. Kids really get a kick out of this.
- Another positive about bowling is that it is available to do in all sorts of weather, but everyone knows that. To avoid being at the bowling alley caught without a lane because the alley got busy on a rainy day, call ahead and reserve one.
- Another fact about bowling that makes it a perfect activity for families is the ability to play as many games as you wish. Each game takes about 20-30 minutes for 4 players and you can play one or as many as your family desires.
- Get information on leagues for kids or adults while you are there.
- Teach your kids proper bowling etiquette when you get to your lane. Have older kids do the scoring.

Resources:

Professional Bowlers Association
http://www.pba.com/
Get some tips from the professionals.

Go Bowling!
http://www.gobowling.com/
Directory of bowling alleys, tips on how to play and more.

County and Local Fairs and Festivals

A taste of the local area can always be found during a county or local fair or festival. If your staycation is at the same time as your local fair, you will need to plan some time to go. Here are tips to help your family enjoy this fun local activity:

- The best time to take kids to the fair is during the time that they sell a discount tags or wristlets for riding the carnival rides. You can save a ton of money by not paying the high ticket prices and going for the all-you-can-ride option.
- Are discount tickets for your local or county fair offered at your local shops? If so, take advantage of the discounts and the fact that you will not have to stand in line when you go.
- Can you take a bus into the fair? If so, it is a viable alternative to driving and trying to find parking.
- Stop at the information booth and find out all that is being offered for the time your family will be there. Ask about free offerings and take advantage of them. Our town in Pennsylvania was the home of an M&M Mars plant. They were always in attendance during the local fair. Their booth handed out candy, for free, every time you walked by. Our family would do so any opportunity we got. Yum, chocolate!
- County and local fairs show of the best of the area. Spend time taking a look at the arts and

crafts. If you have a hobby where you can enter your masterpieces, by all means do so. Not only will it add to your staycation fun, but you will be able to meet new friends who have your same interests and live locally.

- Petting farm animals is another enjoyable activity at local and county fairs. Your kids will be able to see and pet goats, sheep, bunnies and other docile farm animals. You'll want to being your hand sanitizer for the occasion, even though they may have some available.
- Side shows, like the dog tricks show, can be very exciting for the whole family. But you'll want to steer kids away from the 'freaks of nature' type side shows as they can give a child nightmares for life. And even if it isn't that bad, you will still be spending the rest of your staycation explaining how a 'snake-skinned boy' is possible.
- Pass on the carnival food and go to the food stands that offer your local eats. Churches, youth groups and the like often run fundraisers by selling food at county and local fairs. Seek them out and give them your support while satisfying your family's meal needs.

Resources:

Festivals.com
http://www.festivals.com/
Check there directory for a festival or fair near your home.

Local Sporting Events

Sports are fun to attend but to see a major league team is costly for families and it's often impossible to get tickets at the last minute. But, if you have a local college near you, you are in for a treat. They have sports games all of the time that are very exciting to watch and will not break the bank.

Colleges, including community colleges, have home games for every season. Soccer and football are played in the fall as is volleyball and field hockey. Basketball and wrestling are played in the winter. Baseball, softball and track are played in the spring. During the summer colleges often have camps for kids who play sports.

There are some added benefits to college sporting events over the professional. Drinking is not allowed and fans tend to be less crazy or they are asked to leave. Your kids are going to get an up-close experience with a sport as opposed to being so far away you need to use binoculars.

The price is right for these games, often not more than a couple of dollars and your kids may even get in for free if they are local students. You'll want to check out the food policy if it is an indoor event, but bring water and snacks for outdoor sports events. Always plan for it to be colder and wetter outside than you think it will be. If you bring the umbrella and it doesn't rain, no foul, right? But being without it in the rain is no fun for anybody. Also never assume you will have a seat in an outdoor event. Bring a chair or blanket for the whole family to sit on.

Miniature Golf

Miniature golf courses are a fun way for families to spend an evening or afternoon. Normally it takes only a couple of hours to get through all eighteen-holes; less of it's a nine-hole course. They are themed, so be sure to read any signs along the way that add to the experience. Have a dramatic child? Give that job to them.

Much of the fun of mini-golf for families is the friendly competition while playing a game that is easy for even younger children to learn. Then you add in the dips, twists and drops and you realize that with any luck, your children are going to win the game. Mini-golf is a very humbling experience for parents.

You'll want to wear seasonal clothing and be prepared for the weather as the course does not usually close in the rain. Wear comfortable shoes and bring water to drink. Wear hats as there is little shade on the courses.

Put one of your children in charge of keeping score and go over a copy of the rules before you start to play with everyone. Help your little ones get their ball to go where they want it to. If you have all younger children, between the ages of 4 and 9, switch up the game and play whoever gets the most hits at the ball, wins.

Resources:

World Mini-Golf Sport Federation
http://www.minigolfsport.com/
The WMF is the umbrella organization of minigolf sports association's worldwide and continental associations in Asia, Europe and America.

MiniatureGolfCourses.net
http://www.miniaturegolfcourses.net
Find miniature golf courses from around the United States.

Laser Tag

Laser tag is a game where teams go around trying to pick off members of other teams using a light beam gun while wearing a chest piece that will let you know when you have been shot. Often the arena of the game is set in a futuristic world theme. Many times it is a dark arena with neon lights. It is very physical as you run or walk swiftly and hide or pursue other players.

Laser tag is for families who have children that a school-age, 7-year-olds and above. But some laser tag arenas have their own rules and agc limits. There may be a 'kids only' limit as well, so if you are looking to get the whole family into the fun, you'll need an arena that allows all ages at the same time. You will need to call before you go if you think there may be any issues. Boys tend to enjoy this activity more than girls, but it can be played by all.

As this activity is indoors, weather is not a concern. But wearing comfortable clothing to be active in is a must. Many accidents happen because children do not have on proper footwear for jumping and being active.

Go over the rules with the whole family before entering the arena. Remember there are other families there enjoying the fun as well. Safety first will ensure that everyone in your family will enjoy the experience.

Many times there is an arcade with the laser tag arena. Talk about this and set your budget with your kids before you go as this add-on expense can become astronomical.

Outdoor Rock Climbing, Zip lining, Climbing Walls and Ropes Courses

What do all of these activities have in common? They happen up in the air, they are adventurous and active kids love to do them. If you have a household of active kids, you may want to see if you have any area places that offer these activities. Often they are offered near camping areas or at indoor gyms.

Outdoor rock climbing is a great staycation activity for the experienced rock climber if you are just on your own and not hiring a guide. Experience is the key as it can be dangerous. Also, this activity may not be for everyone in the family, you'll want to test it out before your staycation to be sure your family will have a good time. Although, if your family is adventurous and you can find a guide or outdoor rock climbing activity center, give it a try. Often places that offer rock climbing to families also have hiking, rope climbing and zip lining - where you are attached to a harness and zip down a cable way up in the air.

Ropes courses offer special advantages to families as they are used in confidence building and trust building activities for groups. A family who completes a ropes course set of activities set up by those who run the ropes courses will feel more connected to each other and more confident as individuals who each make a part of your family unit. Another worthwhile staycation activity that builds strong family bonds!

*For the best online resources check the state and national parks websites listed under the Visit a State or National Park.

Family Fun Centers

These family fun-time places offer a variety of activities for those who want to get out and enjoy each other while playing games. Here is a list of the activities your local fun center may have:

- Arcade Games
- Redemption Games
- Batting Cages
- Outdoor Go-Karts
- Miniature Golf
- Bumper Cars

- Bumper Boats
- Bowling
- Outdoor Maze
- Inflatables
- Kiddie Rides
- Ride and Sport Simulators
- Shooting Galleries
- Train Rides
- Water Play
- Giant Cranes
- Interactive Games
- Water Games
- Water Rides

If your family has made this one of their activity destinations, you will want to research the facilities. Should this activity be a day trip or just an afternoon or evening activity? That will depend on what is offered at the particular family activity center you are researching. Is there enough to do in the amount of time you have or will your kids get bored? Or the opposite, are you scheduling enough time to do everything your family will want to do at that center?

Another issue when you are researching your local family fun center is to find out the costs. Do they have packages? What are they and what are the prices? You can usually find this out at the center's website, or stop by and ask for a brochure that includes prices. Also, don't be afraid to call and ask them any questions you have – they are the ones with the answers!

Quirky Places

Ever town has got them, from Hub Cap Heaven in Maine to Gatorland in Florida. Odd places that people have just got to see to believe. Many are just odd things people have built for the purpose of selling something, like advertising ketchup by creating the World's Largest Catsup Bottle in Collinsville, Illinois or the Big Duck on Long Island was built in 1930 to sell duck eggs. While these quirky places may not take much of your staycation time, adding your local oddity into the schedule will add just that much more fun – just don't forget your camera!

Resources:

World's Largest Things
http://www.worldslargestthings.com/wllist.htm

Ripley's Museums
http://www.ripleys.com
Ripley Entertainment is the largest and fastest-growing international chain of museum-type tourist attractions in the world.

At-Home Theme Days and Activity Ideas

"There is no doubt that it is around the family and the home that all the greatest virtues, the most dominating virtues of human society, are created, strengthened and maintained." ~ Winston Churchill

Creating a theme for a staycation day will help organize it and will make it special. A theme adds to the excitement of the activity your family will be doing. For instance, beating your siblings at Wii Tennis is fun. But becoming the Ultimate Smith Family Wii Tennis Champion after destroying your sibling competition is something that makes memories. Check out all of the ideas, tips and resources.

Have a Family Video Game Competition

You know those video games you've purchased for holiday and birthday gifts? Pull them out and challenge the rest of your family to a game tournament. If you want to really turn the competition into a staycation event, turn up the excitement by initiating the challenge before the staycation and building the anticipation beforehand. Here are some tips on how to have an exciting video game competition:

- Choose one game that everyone in your family is able to play, like the Wii bowling game.
- After choosing the game, challenge your family to a friendly competition by inviting them with printed invitations that have the time and date on them.
- Check that you have all of the game parts, extra batteries and anything extra that you may need.
- If you have younger children, divide the family up into teams instead of playing as individuals.
- Keep this a budget friendly staycation idea and use what you have on hand. For instance, dress the teams into color t-shirts that you and your family already own.
- Keep snacks and food simple so you can focus on the game and enjoy playing with your family.

Spa Day

No reason to head to an expensive resort for a spa experience. You can create a spa right in your own home. Set the atmosphere with a CD or a few MP3s of relaxing sounds of nature, light some aroma therapy candles and you are on your way. Kids, especially tween and teen girls, enjoy this type of relaxing staycation day. Here are some tips:

- Take an in home yoga class. There are lots of yoga videos online and available to purchase or rent. If you are a beginner, start with free resources and see how much you enjoy it before investing in a yoga CD collection.
- Enjoy a foot bath with tea tree foot soak and then give yourself a pedicure.
- Give yourself a facial. Research your skin type and that of anyone else in your family getting a facial as each person may have different needs. Facials come in single packets at many drug stores or you can make your own with recipes found online.
- Take a long hot bath using scented bath soaps and salts. Block out the rest of the world with relaxing music.
- Use an eye pillow and work through a meditation cd while lying in your living room or bedroom in the dark.
- You'll also want to give yourself a hand massage with scented hand cream and a manicure.

- After all this personal pampering, you'll feel brand new and very relaxed.

Resources:

Homemade Facials and Face Masks
http://www.wittyliving.com/recipes/facial-mask-recipes.html
I have a large list of make your own facials offered here.

A Hobby Day

Any hobbyist can tell you that there aren't enough hours in the day or days in the week to enjoy the hobby that they love. So why not plan a day in your staycation for the hobbyists in your family to enjoy what they love doing. Here are tips on how:

- Inform your family that you will be having a hobby day during your staycation. You will need a list of what they may need to work on their hobby for that day.
- If your kids are older, ask them to plan out the day so that they know what they want to do and can tell you what they need on their own. If you have a young child, help them plan some time to work on a project that they have the ability to do all by themselves or with minimal help. If they are unable to do activities on their own, think about hiring a teenager to come play with them while you work on your hobby that day. You will need to have the activities ready for

them to do, but you do not have to be the one to do it. Remember that it is your staycation as well.

- Place a budget on each person's hobby supplies so that no one eats up all of your staycation funds.
- If there is a new hobby the whole family would like to try, by all means try it!

Learn to Cook Something New

Not too long ago, I was a part of a cooking class given in a specialty store. It wasn't for anything too fancy, but I have to say I loved the experience. If you are like me and you enjoy playing and creating in your kitchen as well as using it as a tool to get your family fed, then this staycation activity is right up your alley.

Now, let's take a minute and talk about your budget as this activity can cost you next to nothing or quite a bit of money. If you are looking to try something like a new dish or a new type of cooking and it takes no new tools for your kitchen, then the food you purchase comes out of your food expenses, which is not really a staycation expense as you would be cooking and feeding your family anyway. That said, if you do need to purchase a tool, like say a Wok, for this staycation activity, don't shy away from doing it because of the purchase. Yes, it ups the staycation budget, but it is a purchase you will use over and over again.

If you have preteens and teens, take this opportunity to share you love of cooking. Ask what type of foods they would like to try and make and you can create something together. Or they can make a side to your main dish.

If the food is something that is too sophisticated for the younger people in your family, offer them something that they will enjoy instead. Kids don't always like to test their taste buds like adults do. Give them the choice to try the new food, but have a backup.

Have a Do-Nothing, Pajama or Time-Out Day

A pajama day is my family's favorite way to spend an unexpected day off. Can't go anywhere or do anything because the weather is too bad? Put on your slippers, kickback and do nothing of any consequence. Enjoy the non-planned day where you can play a board game if you want to, read the comics or take a nap. Teens love it because they can sleep in until noon.

Some families enjoy this type of day as a planned staycation day. They call it their Time-Out or Do-Nothing Day. They plan it out and have food and activities ready. They can chose to sleep in late or get up early to read in the quiet of the morning.

When you have a 'do nothing' type of day, you will need to plan activities for younger kids that they can do on their own. I have always found it best to keep these activities a surprise and something that I know they will really enjoy. I, like many moms, know that the busier you keep younger children, the happier they are and thereby the happier everyone else is.

I find this type of staycation day is great when following a busier day trip day, especially if you drive back to your home late the night before. Then sleeping in the next morning during your PJ Day is a wonderfully relaxing idea.

Enjoy an All Day Movie Marathon

Watching movies all day is a fantasy staycation for many genre movie fans or for those families that have favorite movies and television shows they like to watch in blocks of time. My husband and I enjoy watching Lost in full season runs. But our kids would enjoy seeing High School Musical 1, 2 and 3 a million times more. There are just so many possibilities that you may have to schedule one of these into your family's schedule every month or so whether or not you are having a staycation. Here are some tips to make your All Day Movie Marathon a success:

- Movies can run from a series like Harry Potter to everyone being able to pick their favorite movie and titling the day The ______ Family's Favorite Movie Marathon on your staycation schedule.
- Watch the age limit on some movies as you will not want younger children to be exposed to things that are not age appropriate or too scary for them. If you would like to see a movie that

is for the older crowd, show it last after the kids have gone to bed.

- Run with the movie going theme and buy popcorn bags to fill, single serving boxes of gummy candies or chocolate and give everyone a ticket.
- Make the family movie area comfy with pillows, blankets and cozy chairs.
- Popcorn is the snack of choice for many movie watchers, but you can also stock up on nachos and cheese or movie candies like non-perils.
- Enjoy a fun game of movie trivia after you finish a movie and try to stump each other. Or you can write up a Q&A movie trivia game and give prizes to the one who has the most correct answers.

Resources:

Movies @ About.com
http://movies.about.com

Netflix.com
http://netflix.com

Spend the Day Enjoying Your Own Pool

If you have a pool in your backyard, you have the makings of a fun filled staycation day without having to leave home. You can plan a day with the kids enjoying the warm weather and their laughter. Here are some tips:

- Before you get started, remind everyone about your pool safety rules. Read them allowed so that they are clear in everyone's mind. You want to have a good time on this staycation day, not spend it in the hospital with a child getting stitches or worse.
- Create a theme around your pool day and plan your menu around it. For instance, if your pool day is around Independence Day, make a red, white and blue fruit salad out of strawberries, blueberries and mini-marshmallows.
- Play games! Beach ball or water volleyball, Marko polo and a penny toss are all games kids enjoy and you will have fun playing too. Even if it's just you and the kids, playing games with family is fun. Have a water balloon toss or a water gun fight with super soakers.
- Keep the menu simple. Pull out your order-in menus from local restaurants, pull out a ready-made cold cut platter or heat hot dogs on the grill.
- Inflatable boats, toys and floatable items add to the fun for kids who know how to swim. You can even have silly races with tubes and other swimming toys. Also if you have toddlers, purchase a small inflatable pool for the day's fun.
- Create an inviting outdoor rest area. Using outdoor pillows and lounge chairs you can make an area for sleepy kids to rest outside, instead of having to go in and change before napping.

Go Hawaiian for the Day

Hawaiian is always a fun theme which is easy to pull off as most party stores carry supplies for the theme in ample quantity. It is also a great theme day for extended family get-togethers. Here are some tips

- Decorate with grass table skirts and Hawaiian flowers and leis.
- Dress the part with grass skirts and leis for a necklace, bracelet and in your hair.
- Learn how to hula by watching a video the morning of the luau. Then enjoy some hula dancing with music at your family luau.
- Scented candles with the scent of the Islands will help transform the atmosphere.
- You can have a Hawaiian Luau for your main meal of the day.
- Coconuts make for fun cups that you can drink fruit drinks for the kids and cocktails for the adults. Be sure you have a sharp enough knife to cut open the top or purchase them that day and get your grocery to cut them for you.
- Serve fresh tropical fruits on a skewer like pineapple, kiwi and mangos. Use flavored yogurt for a dip.
- Grill some ham and pineapple slices and serve with a baked potato for a quick and easy meal.
- Coconut battered chicken tenders with mustard or barbecue dips. Have some authentic poi, if you enjoy the taste.

- Water and pool games are fun activities during a luau or get a nice long stick and do the limbo. Who can go the lowest in your family? Who needs to get more limber? It's nice if you have the limbo music, as well. You can find the song on iTunes or other MP3 stores.

Family Themed Parties resources and information can be found at http://familyfun.go.com/parties/ and http://entertaining.about.com

Adding Adults-Only Time to Your Staycation

Rejuvenating during a vacation means you will want to spend time with your spouse and enjoy time as a couple. If you can fit an extra day into your vacation schedule, do so. If not, think about using one of the days you have or even just an afternoon if that is all you can get. Call it your Adults-Only Time.

You do not have to share with anyone what you are doing – except perhaps your spouse. Give the kids a day away from mom and dad by sending them off with friends or extended family. If you have friends who also have children, offer to switch kids the next time they want time alone.

Use the time to reconnect to each other and not talk about what your kids are doing or how work has been going. Go for a walk, hold hands, set up some romance. Simply enjoy the wonderful relationship you are in.

The More You Staycation, The More You Will Want to Staycation

"*No man needs a vacation so much as the person who has just had one.*" ~Elbert Hubbard

Today's family spends a lot of time on the go, more so than any generation that came before us. Both dads and moms are working, sometimes more than one job. Kids are in school or daycares all day long. Everyone comes home at night tired, but the schedule continues to be packed with club meetings, the kids sport events and social networking on the computer. This makes for a family that is too busy to enjoy each other and what they have. A staycation will give you the ability to and an appreciation of both. And when you do get the self-satisfaction of enjoying the relaxation you can have right in your own home, you are going to want to do that more and more.

Another added benefit to having a family staycation: You will learn to appreciate your local area and what it has to offer your family in terms of entertainment, fitness and culture. You will find new things to do more often as there is a wealth of things for your family to enjoy and appreciate in your local area. You simply need the time it takes to ferret out which things you like to do and which are not your family's cup of tea.

In my humble opinion, this is what staycations do best for families. Staycations help families spend more time with each other throughout the whole year, not just during the staycation. Sure they save money and tone down my stress level because you're not dealing with air travel. But the fact is they open up an entire world in our own backyard – really, including our backyards. We get to enjoy this world with our kids. It's amazing. We don't always see this because we are too busy with work, school, kids' sports and activities, etc. But a staycation helps point it all out and creates a solution.

Once you and your family have a positive experience during your staycation, you'll want to do that again. Say for instance, your family decides to try eating at a Japanese restaurant complete with a chef that cuts and twirls food around while he prepares it in front of you. You all have a wonderful time. Then a couple of months go by and you want to do something fun with your family, now you know that everyone likes the Japanese place. Perfect time to do that again!

It isn't a myth that the more you do something the easier it seems to do and the more benefits you will reap from it. It has its base in the reasons behind forming habits and gaining experiences. When you get used to doing something or an idea, it becomes easier to do in your mind and you will become more positive about it. In turn you will look for more positive outcomes, etc. All the while this is happening for you, it's happening for your family as well. Your kids will talk about the memories, the next day you have off they will ask to something fun at home together, it will snowball and strengthen your family bonds.

Saving Staycation Memories

Take lots of pictures as you go places and do things. Keep your camera out on the counter where it is easy to grab and snap a few shots of the family playing a board game. Take posed shots and wacky pictures as well. I have one with my then 4-year-old dancing around with a game piece that spelled the word LIFE stuck on her forehead. I'm saving that photo for her wedding video.

The weekend following your staycation, get your pictures printed out and place them in a photo album. Put the album on the table in the family room for those who are there to add notes to the pictures or just look at the fun time that you had. While having the pictures on a memory card is fun too, having the pictures will allow you to keep them for a very long time. You may even be able to share them with your grandchildren.

Begin Planning Your Next Staycation

Even if you next family staycation is a year away, it will be easy to plan if you start now because you have all of the information you need right in front of you. Plus, the memories are fresh in everyone's mind and you will want to get your family's opinions.

________________ Family Staycation Survey

What was your favorite activity? Why?
What was your least favorite activity? Why?
Where would you like to go or what would you like to do again? Name three.

1.
2.
3.

What other things would you like to do on our next staycation? Name three.

1.
2.
3.

Organize the flyers and other printed information in a safe place where you can pull it out when you want to start planning again. Do not keep everything because you'll forget what you liked and what you didn't. So, purge everything you didn't use if it was not brought up on the surveys.

Appendix: State Park Websites

Alabama
http://www.alapark.com/
Alaska
http://www.dnr.state.ak.us/parks/
Arizona
http://www.azstateparks.com/
Arkansas
http://www.arkansasstateparks.com/
California
http://www.parks.ca.gov/
Colorado
http://www.parks.state.co.us/
Connecticut
http://www.ct.gov/dep/site/default.asp
Delaware
http://www.destateparks.com/
Florida
http://www.floridastateparks.org/
Georgia
http://www.gadnr.org/
Hawaii
http://www.hawaiistateparks.org/
Idaho
http://parksandrecreation.idaho.gov/
Illinois
http://dnr.state.il.us/lands/landmgt/parks/
Indiana
http://www.in.gov/dnr/parklake/
Iowa
http://www.iowa.gov/state/main/index.html
Kansas
http://www.kdwp.state.ks.us/
Kentucky
http://parks.ky.gov/
Louisiana
http://www.crt.state.la.us/
Maine
http://www.state.me.us/doc/parks/
Maryland
http://www.dnr.state.md.us/publiclands/

Massachusetts
http://www.mass.gov/dcr/forparks.htm
Michigan
http://www.michigan.gov/dnr
Minnesota http://www.dnr.state.mn.us/state_parks/index.html
Mississippi
http://home.mdwfp.com/
Missouri
http://www.mostateparks.com/
Montana
http://fwp.mt.gov/parks/default.html
Nebraska
http://www.ngpc.state.ne.us/
Nevada
http://parks.nv.gov/
New Hampshire
http://www.nhparks.state.nh.us/
New Jersey
http://www.state.nj.us/dep/parksandforests/
New Mexico
http://www.emnrd.state.nm.us/PRD/
New York
http://nysparks.com/
North Carolina
http://www.ncparks.gov/Visit/main.php
North Dakota
http://www.ndparks.com/
Ohio
http://www.ohiostateparks.org
Oklahoma
http://www.touroklahoma.com/
Oregon
http://egov.oregon.gov/OPRD/index.shtml
Pennsylvania
http://www.dcnr.state.pa.us/stateparks/
Rhode Island
http://www.riparks.com/
South Carolina
http://www.southcarolinaparks.com/
South Dakota
http://gfp.sd.gov/state-parks/
Tennessee
http://www.state.tn.us/environment/parks/

Texas
http://www.tpwd.state.tx.us/spdest/
Utah
http://stateparks.utah.gov/stateparks/
Vermont
http://www.vtstateparks.com/
Virginia
http://www.dcr.virginia.gov/
Washington
http://www.parks.wa.gov/
West Virginia
http://www.wvparks.com/
Wisconsin
http://www.dnr.state.wi.us/org/land/parks/
Wyoming
http://wyoparks.state.wy.us/

Index

A

B

C

D

F

R

S

T

V

W

www.ingramcontent.com/pod-product-compliance
Ingram Content Group UK Ltd.
Pitfield, Milton Keynes, MK11 3LW, UK
UKHW040601210726
13854UKWH00008B/1705